TAMING
the
LION

*Overcoming the Obstacles
to Associational Excellence*

Alma, thank you for reminding me that ideas need to be shared!

by B.R. Rick Curtis, PhD
introduction by Hugh Townsend

Title: Taming the Lion: Overcoming the Obstacles to Associational Excellence
Author: B.R. Rick Curtis, PhD
© 2024 North American Mission Board. All Rights Reserved.
ISBN: 978-1-304-30647-0
Release date: February 2024. Most recently updated: May 2024

Published by The North American Mission Board of the Southern Baptist Convention, Inc.
Alpharetta, Georgia

Contents

Introduction

James D. (Murph) Murphy, a former F-15 fighter pilot during the Iraq war and other military operations, offers a compelling analogy in his book *Business is Combat*: "There's an expression in the fighter pilot community – we call ourselves the pointy end of the spear. It's a bit braggadocio, but there's something to it; we actually believe that our organization, the United States Air Force, is like a spear, and as the first players into the theater of battle, we fighter pilots constitute its sharp-edged tip. All the functions within this vast, geographically dispersed 'corporation' of 700,000 employees are narrowly behind one thing – our missions. There's no empire building, no bickering, no politics, just one question to be asked: is what we're doing serving to make the pilots more successful in their missions? From research and development to weathermen, everyone has to answer the same question: will what we are doing contribute to the success of the mission?"

Applying this scenario to the local church and the Baptist association raises a critical question. In this analogy, local churches are the pointy end of the spear, directly engaging with the world and the cultures in which they exist. Conversely, the association serves in the role of the United States Air Force and must therefore ask the question: is what we are doing serving to make our churches successful in their mission?

In this eloquently written book by Rick Curtis, he addresses critical questions and issues that face the Baptist associations as they define and seek to fulfill their role. Rick makes a major distinction in chapter seven, indicating that the association is not a church. Thus, it is imperative for the association to clearly define who they are and what their mission is.

There is no question we live in challenging times. As a result, Rick addresses seven issues the association faces as it strives to move forward and serve as a successful resource to their churches. Each chapter is filled with both challenges and a multitude of practical suggestions to assist the association in providing both adequate and appropriate resources to support local congregations as they seek to be the pointy end of the spear in their community. Every chapter is relevant for today's association. Virtually every association is faced with limited resources. Rick provides excellent avenues for the association to develop partnerships to expand their resource base. It's not enough to simply have resources; the challenge is to have the right resources to assist the churches. This not only means financial resources but also personnel resources, including a volunteer base that can bring a wealth of experience and expertise to the churches.

Perhaps one of the greatest challenges for the association relates to missional alignment. This involves knowing who you are and why you exist. Clarifying these two things allows the association to bring relevance to its churches. In chapter six, Rick references what has been called the "Four F's." The third and fourth "F" are focused and friendly. Focused relates to missional alignment, and friendly raises the question: is the association the first place churches go to find resource help? Missional alignment is critical if the association is to remain relevant to its churches.

Several years ago, when I was addressing the concept of mission drift, I came across this example. Missions are often subtle, like boiling a frog. One author said, "Be mean about the vision; don't compromise who you are and the mission you have been called to." A classic, yet tragic, illustration is the mission statement for Harvard. The statement is "Everyone shall consider as the main end of his life and studies, to know God and Jesus Christ, which is eternal life." Do you think there has been any mission drift at Harvard?

Chapter six addresses the issue of adapting to change. We have heard it said all our lives, there are two things that are inevitable – death and taxes. The third leg of that statement should include change. It is inevitable! In his book *Deep Change*, Robert Quinn says, "Change or die." Unless the association is continually evaluating its effectiveness, it can quickly become outdated and thus irrelevant to its churches. Again, Rick provides concrete suggestions for maintaining relevance and how to address the elephant of change.

Taming the Lion is not to be read as a novel or a fictional book. It is a resource book that you can refer to repeatedly. As you face any of the challenges addressed in this book, go back, and review the foundational principles. Again, Rick provides a multitude of practical ideas and help.

Thank you, Rick, for such a timely and excellent work. I wholeheartedly endorse this book and pray that it will be used to make an impact for the kingdom of God as associations across this country re-vision their mission and purpose.

Dr. Hugh G. Townsend
HMB/NAMB Association Missions Division. 1990 - 2013

Preface

Amidst the profound call to serve and the steadfast commitment to faith, Baptist associations across these United States of America find themselves at a pivotal juncture, navigating an increasingly complex landscape of sustainability challenges. From stewardship of resources to the preservation of community, these associations stand as pillars of hope and support for their congregations and the communities they serve. Yet, as the world contends with geopolitical crises, economic disparities, evolving self-identities, theological ignorance or redefinitions, and shifting societal dynamics, the challenge of securing a sustainable future for these associations has never been more urgent. In this book, I delve into the intricate tapestry of sustainability challenges facing Baptist associations, exploring the intersections of faith, leadership, and stewardship in charting a course toward a resilient and thriving future.

The Baptist association stands as a relevant and relational pillar for the pastors and lay leaders whom it serves, embodying the timeless values of faith, compassion, and service. Rooted in the rich tradition of Baptist principles, these associations are steadfast in their commitment to infecting their member churches with the unquenchable desire for excellence, integrity, spirituality, and efficiency. With a focus on empowering their member churches to live out their mission in tangible ways, Baptist associations foster a sense of belonging and unity among their members, nurturing a vibrant community where everyone is valued and welcomed. Through their tireless efforts in building the faith community, education, and advocacy, these associations play a vital role in addressing pressing social issues, uplifting those who are called to ministry, and promoting the importance of community engagement with the Good News of Jesus Christ. With unwavering dedication and unwavering faith, the Baptist association continues to be a force for good, inspiring hearts and transforming leaders one church at a time.

Furthermore, the spiritual depth and wisdom of the associational mission strategist serves as the guiding light that sets the tone for member churches within the association. These leaders, grounded in their faith and equipped with a wealth of spiritual and practical knowledge, inspire and empower congregations to deepen their own spiritual journeys. By exemplifying integrity, humility, and a genuine commitment to serving God and others, associational leaders foster a culture of spiritual growth and maturity within the broader faith community. Their wisdom informs decision-making, their compassion fuels unity, and their steadfast faith serves as a beacon of hope in times of uncertainty. As spiritual shepherds, associational leaders not only lead by example but also nurture a collective spirit of purpose and reverence for God's calling, thereby shaping the ethos and character of member churches.

Many have heard me say over the years that the most important entity in the SBC ecosystem (save the local church) is the local Baptist association. My years as the associational mission strategist at the High Desert Baptist Association in California proved to be formative, enlightening, and immeasurably satisfying. It was a position of honor, to be able to walk with a man of God through the difficulties presented to him and to be his armor bearer as he conquered his present reality and glorified the Father in the process. Brothers, it does not get any better than that! This book is dedicated to you, man of God, as you lead your association with excellence.

B.R. Rick Curtis

01
Taming the Lion

For God is not unjust; he will not forget your work and the love you demonstrated for his name by serving the saints—and by continuing to serve them. Now we desire each of you to demonstrate the same diligence for the full assurance of your hope until the end, so that you won't become lazy but will be imitators of those who inherit the promises through faith and perseverance.

Hebrews 6:10-12

I remember a story told when I was young, about a fierce lion that could not be tamed. I never knew why he was so fierce, and as a child it didn't really matter. Perhaps it was because of the many expectations placed upon him as the king of the jungle, or because he was overwhelmed at the many obstacles that stood between him and harmony in the kingdom. Perhaps it was a manifestation of his emotional strife and his lack of close relationships with the other animals, or the jealousy of what all the other animals could achieve. However, these are the thoughts of a leader looking back at a beloved childhood story. Nevertheless, the story does have application to the many issues that work against a quality association and speaks also to the importance of the wise and steadfast associational mission strategist that every association needs. Allow me to share my remembered version of the children's story told to me so long ago, and then share with you what I have come to believe are the seven main reasons why the lion is so hard to tame. Here is the story…

Once upon a time, in a lush African savannah, there lived a majestic lion named Shida. Shida was not like any other lion; he was known far and wide for his wild and uncontrollable nature. His roar echoed across the plains, striking fear into the hearts of animals big and small. No one dared to challenge him, for he ruled his territory with an iron paw.

However, Shida's ferocity often caused trouble for the other inhabitants of the savannah. His unpredictable behavior led to conflicts with other animals, disrupting the delicate balance of life in the wilderness. The elders of the animal kingdom grew concerned, fearing that Shida's reign of terror would bring chaos and despair to their once peaceful home.

One day, a wise old elephant named Busara decided to intervene. Busara had seen enough suffering caused by Shida's rampage and knew that something had to be done. With a determined spirit and a heart full of compassion, Busara set out on a mission to tame the unruly lion.

Busara approached Shida with caution, mindful of the danger that lay ahead. The lion's fierce gaze met Busara's steady eyes, and for a moment, the savannah fell silent. But instead of lashing out in anger, Shida hesitated, sensing something different in Busara's presence.

With patience and perseverance, Busara began to build a bond with Shida, earning his trust one step at a time. Busara showed Shida kindness and understanding, teaching him the value of empathy and cooperation. Slowly but surely, the once untamable lion began to change.

Under Busara's guidance, Shida learned to channel his strength and courage for the greater good. He became a protector of the weak and a guardian of the land, using his mighty roar to warn others of impending danger. No longer a threat to the harmony of the savannah, Shida became a symbol of hope and redemption.

As the days passed, Shida's transformation inspired others to overcome their fears and prejudices. The animals of the savannah learned to live in harmony, embracing diversity and unity as they worked together to build a better future for the savannah. They teamed up to face every challenge, and because of their unity, those challenges were conquered.

And so, the tale of the once unmanageable lion who was tamed by the wisdom and compassion of a wise old elephant became a legend, reminding all who heard it of the power of love, wisdom, patience, and teamwork to transform even the most formidable of challenges.

As you are aware, the local Baptist association has its challenges. It needs a Busara to bring stability to its chaos. It is an anomaly. It does not receive cooperative program dollars and must therefore find the ability to stand on its own. Some may disagree with what I am about to say, but here goes: the absence of cooperative dollars is an advantage. It is an advantage because the local association has the challenge, yet ability, to be the most relevant organization in the life of a pastor. Its marching orders are its own and free from the SBC Executive Committee's ministry assignments. That being said, it takes work to be relevant and on point. Everyone has an opinion on what the association should be doing. Not only that, but there are also forces—inherent to autonomous agencies— that work against their ability to thrive. I want to address seven of those forces and try to provide a framework for discussion at the local level that will help your association. I hope this book serves as your catalytic spark for ideas that will assist you in thinking through some issues that you may not have considered. You may not consider your association a reckless, out of control lion, but it might still be wild. I do know that it needs a Busara to bring balance. A loving, compassionate, strong, truth-telling, strategic, self-sacrificing, driven, and relational Busara to step up and tame the lion.

Let us start with my assumptions. Baptist associations face a unique set of leadership challenges due to their reliance on limited resources, a volunteer-driven workforce, and the complexity of their mission. Some of the biggest challenges are related to stakeholders and their desire to see value in the association. Other challenges are "Leadership 101" issues: adaptation to and the implementation of change, the quality measuring of impact, and the importance of leadership succession.

Addressing these challenges requires strong leadership, strategic thinking, collaboration, and a deep commitment to the organization's mission and values. Effective leaders in the non-profit associational sector must be able to inspire and mobilize others, build strong relationships, and navigate complexity with resilience and creativity. I pray that I may help you think through these issues and come out on top.

This book is designed to serve as more than just a one-time read; it is intended to be a lasting resource for continuous reference as your association evolves. I hope that readers will return to its pages time and again to find guidance and insights as they navigate the issues described within. By revisiting the practical suggestions and foundational principles outlined in this book, leaders can adapt to new challenges and ensure their strategies remain aligned with the association's mission. This enduring resource aims to support ongoing growth and development, helping associations remain effective and relevant in their service to their congregations.

02

Resource Constraints

And God is able to make every grace overflow to you, so that in every way, always having everything you need, you may excel in every good work.

2 Corinthians 9:8

In the now dilapidated city of Lumina, there lived a young man named Milo, whose heart was filled with a burning desire to make a difference in the lives of the city's underprivileged. Milo dreamed of starting a community center in his neighborhood—a place where children could receive education, families could access resources, and individuals could find support in times of need. However, Milo faced a formidable obstacle: he lacked the resources to turn his vision into reality.

Undeterred by the daunting challenge ahead, Milo set out on a journey of determination and resilience. He began by reaching out to local businesses, sharing his vision for the community center and appealing for their support. Despite facing rejection and skepticism from many, Milo refused to give up, believing wholeheartedly in the transformative power of his idea.

As Milo continued to pursue his dream, he encountered unexpected allies along the way. A small group of volunteers rallied to his cause, offering their time, skills, and resources to help bring his vision to life. Together, they organized fundraisers, community events, and awareness campaigns, spreading the word about Milo's project and inspiring others to get involved.

Despite the challenges and setbacks they faced, Milo and his team pressed on with unwavering determination. They reached out to government agencies, philanthropic organizations, and community leaders, seeking additional support and resources for their cause. Slowly but surely, their efforts began to bear fruit as donations, grants, and in-kind contributions poured in, providing the necessary funds, materials, and support to turn Milo's vision into reality.

Finally, after months of tireless effort and perseverance, Milo stood proudly before the newly opened community center—a beacon of hope and opportunity for the people of Lumina. With tears of joy in his eyes, Milo thanked his supporters, volunteers, and allies who had helped him overcome every obstacle and hurdle along the way. And as the doors of the community center swung open, Milo knew that his dream had become a reality—a testament to the power of determination, resilience, and belief in the possibility of creating positive change in the world.

Baptist associations, like many non-profit organizations, often operate with limited budgets, inadequate volunteers, and diminishing resources, requiring them to be resourceful and strategic in order to maximize their impact. Many face the daunting challenge of having to scratch and scrape for everything they need to fulfill their vision. This struggle can hinder their ability to fulfill their missions effectively. With limited funding streams, they must contend with rising costs, increased demand for services, and unforeseen emergencies. These organizations rely heavily on donations, grants, and volunteer support to sustain their operations and initiatives. However, economic fluctuations, shifting donor priorities, and competition for funding with other organizations can create uncertainty and instability. As resources dwindle, associations are forced to make difficult decisions, often prioritizing certain programs over others, or scaling back on essential services. The most common tragedy is found in a budget that is strained and a decision is made to support staff salary resulting in very little—or no—ministry budget. The constant pressure to do more with less can strain staff morale and compromise the quality and reach of their programs. Despite these challenges, most associations demonstrate remarkable resilience and ingenuity, continually seeking innovative solutions and partnerships to maximize their impact in the face of adversity. Below are ten strategies to assist you in starting conversations and developing resource solutions.

Strategic Planning

Develop a clear strategic plan that outlines organizational goals, priorities, and strategies for achieving them. This plan should prioritize activities that align with the organization's mission and have the greatest potential for impact. Most people will not give their support to the undefined. In the marketplace of ideas and action, you need to provide a clear, concise plan to build confidence and trust for the stakeholder. Pastors live in a world in which they understand their people and know that every person in the pew wants to trust that his or her gift will be used for kingdom purposes. What are the association's purposes? How will the association achieve them? What are the indicators of success? Strategic planning and clear objectives will win the trust of your people and form a base on which people can give.

Partnerships and Collaboration

Forge partnerships with other non-profits, businesses, government agencies, and community organizations to share resources, expertise, and networks. Collaborating with others can help amplify the impact of limited resources, empower ministry, and reach a broader audience. Unfortunately, there has been a reluctance for associations to work with other associations or state conventions. We see this same reluctance in the local church. Churches don't work with each other for fear of their people liking the other church better. Considering God's sovereignty, this territorial fear is absurd. There are valuable resources in your faith community that can accentuate your associational mission. You simply need to look for them. Here are some easy examples of how partnering can be a win for your people and even inspire them to give financially and of themselves.

Disaster Relief Efforts: Baptist associations often join forces during times of disaster to provide relief efforts. They pool resources such as food, water, shelter, and medical aid to respond effectively to natural disasters, humanitarian crises, and community emergencies. By coordinating their efforts, Baptist associations can reach more people in need and provide comprehensive support to affected communities. When you partner together, you give your churches the ability to participate in something "larger than self" which always pays dividends.

Mission Trips and Outreach Programs: Baptist associations frequently organize mission trips and outreach programs to serve communities locally, nationally, and internationally. By working together, they can share logistical support, transportation, and financial resources to fund these initiatives. This collaborative approach allows the churches of the association to engage in a wider range of outreach activities and reach more people with their message of hope and compassion.

Training and Development Programs: Baptist associations often collaborate with other agencies or individuals to offer training and development programs for pastors, church leaders, and volunteers. These programs may include workshops, conferences, seminars, and online resources covering topics such as leadership development, ministry skills, and pastoral care. By pooling their expertise and resources, Baptist associations can provide high-quality training opportunities that benefit churches and individuals across multiple regions. As the associational mission strategist, you have the ability to bring in some nationally recognized speakers who can utilize their own budgets to inspire your people. (Hint: like the author of this book.)

Community Service Projects: Baptist associations frequently empower local churches and other supportive organizations to undertake community service projects that address social, economic, and environmental needs. These projects may include food drives, clothing drives, neighborhood clean-up efforts, and affordable housing initiatives. By working together, associational churches can leverage their collective resources and networks to make a greater impact in their communities and improve the quality of life for those in need, thus laying the groundwork for member churches to bring gospel conversations to the needy.

Convention Partnerships: Baptist associations often collaborate with larger convention entities, such as state conventions or national organizations, to amplify their efforts and resources. These partnerships may involve sharing funding, expertise, and best practices to support mission work, church planting efforts, and ministry initiatives. By aligning their efforts with convention priorities and strategies, Baptist associations can maximize their effectiveness and contribute to the broader mission of the convention.

I would be remiss if I did not offer a caution at this point. The last thing an association can afford is a sense that the association is competing with the local church. There is no greater way to lose the involvement of your churches than to compete with them. An associational mission strategist must walk a careful line between providing ministry and supporting local church ministries. The association is not a church and should avoid any ministry that belongs to the church. A classic example of this conflict of interest might be a regional evangelism outreach. The astute associational mission strategist will work with a local church to empower that church to hold the event as opposed to "doing" the event and asking the churches to get involved. More on this in chapter nine, "The Association is not a Church."

Volunteer Engagement

Effectively engage and leverage volunteers to supplement paid staff and carry out essential tasks. Volunteers can contribute their time, skills, and passion to support the organization's mission, often at a lower cost than hiring additional staff. If the associational mission strategist is wise, he can tap into the intrinsic motivators found within every individual to purpose them for a task, and he or she will gladly complete the task or ministry without cost to the association. As Daniel Pink has eloquently shown, people are motivated by autonomy, mastery, and purpose.[1] The associational mission strategist that taps into one or more of these areas in the volunteer can all but assure loyal, inexhaustible involvement. I will speak in detail about volunteers in the following chapter.

Technology and Automation

Far be it for me to extol the virtues of a global pandemic, but we all must admit that the events of 2020 accelerated the learning curve related to technology. Every association should invest in cost-effective technologies and tools to streamline processes, improve efficiency, and reduce administrative overhead. This could include using free or low-cost software for project management, communication, fundraising, and data management. Think through each of these recommendations and how they might drive your association to the next level with little or no budgetary impact.

Online Communication Platforms: Utilize free or low-cost communication platforms like email newsletters, social media channels, and messaging apps to stay connected with member churches, pastors, and volunteers. These platforms can be used to share updates, prayer requests, event invitations, and ministry resources, fostering community and collaboration without the need for expensive communication tools.

Virtual Meetings and Training: Most associations now have this handled, but instead of hosting in-person meetings or training events, Baptist associations can utilize free video conferencing tools like Microsoft Teams, Zoom, Google Meet, or Skype to conduct virtual gatherings.

---

1. Daniel H. Pink, *Drive: The Surprising Truth about What Motivates Us.* (New York, NY: Riverhead Books, 2009).

These platforms allow participants to join remotely from anywhere with an internet connection, reducing travel costs and increasing accessibility for members across different locations.

Online Resource Libraries: Create a centralized online repository or resource library where member churches can access sermons, Bible studies, worship music, and other ministry resources for free or at a nominal cost. Utilize platforms like Google Drive, Dropbox, or a church website to organize and share these resources, empowering churches to enhance their ministries without additional expenses. Pastors like Andy Addis of CrossPoint Church in Hutchinson, Kansas, have done an amazing job at providing resources for church replanting to anyone who needs them.[2]

Social Media Outreach: Leverage social media platforms like Facebook, X, Instagram, and YouTube to reach a wider audience and engage with community members. If you are at a loss as to how the association can begin to leverage social media toward resource development, you might start by asking a 14-year-old! They grasp the impact of social media (unfortunately) much better than most associational mission strategists. For starters, consider the following.

> Share Inspiring Content: Post leadership bites, testimonies of associational impact, and event announcements to foster meaningful connections and spread the association's message of excellence and pastoral support. Encourage churches and volunteers to actively participate in online discussions and share their own stories of faith to amplify the association's ministry impact. Use social media platforms such as Facebook, X,

---

2. "Replant Hub," Replant Hub, North American Mission Board, http://replanthub.com.

Instagram, and LinkedIn to share inspirational messages, major breakthroughs, church victories, and measurable advancements. Post regular updates that uplift and encourage your stakeholders to have deeper confidence in the efficiency of the association.

Promote Events and Activities: Announce upcoming events, workshops, seminars, conferences, and community outreach initiatives on social media platforms. Create event pages for your churches, share event details, and encourage members to RSVP and invite their friends, family, and colleagues. By adding this additional support, you drive relevance of the association in the eyes of its pastors.

Facilitate Engagement and Discussion: Initiate conversations and discussions on social media by posing thought-provoking questions, sharing polls, and soliciting feedback from followers. Encourage interaction and dialogue among members, allowing them to share their insights, experiences, and prayer requests.

Highlight Ministries and Testimonials: Showcase the ministries, outreach efforts, and mission projects of member churches and volunteers on social media. Share success stories, impact reports, and testimonials that demonstrate the tangible ways in which the associational churches are making a difference in the lives of individuals and communities.

Foster Community and Connection: Create online groups or communities on platforms like Facebook or LinkedIn where members can connect, support each other, and share resources and prayer requests. Facilitate meaningful interactions and build a sense of belonging and camaraderie among member churches.

Utilize Live Streaming and Video Content: Take advantage of live-streaming features on platforms like Facebook Live, Instagram Live, and YouTube to broadcast associational meetings and special events in real-time. Additionally, create short video clips, testimonials, and interviews to engage followers and convey impactful messages.

Advertise and Amplify Outreach Efforts: Use social media advertising tools to promote specific ministry initiatives in your churches, fundraising campaigns, or outreach events to a targeted audience. Boost posts to reach a wider demographic and maximize the visibility of the association's mission and activities.

Host a podcast: A podcast can serve as a dynamic and engaging tool within a Baptist association to foster increased buy-in from its members. By offering a platform for increased familiarity with associational personalities, introductions to member church staff and ministry personnel, and discussions on relevant theological and community issues, the podcast can enhance a sense of connection and involvement among listeners. It provides a convenient and accessible way for members to stay informed and have a sense of connection to the association, even if they cannot attend every meeting. Moreover, featuring interviews with church leaders and laypersons can build a sense of community and shared purpose, highlighting personal stories and collective goals that resonate with the audience. This ongoing communication helps to reinforce the association's mission and values, encouraging greater participation and commitment from its members.

By leveraging technology in these practical ways, Baptist associations can maximize their ministry impact, enhance communication and collaboration, and empower member churches to fulfill their mission without incurring significant costs.

Creative Fundraising

Explore diverse fundraising strategies beyond traditional methods like grants and donations. This could include hosting events, selling merchandise, crowdfunding campaigns, online auctions, and peer-to-peer fundraising. Baptist associations can also leverage social media and digital marketing to expand their reach and attract supporters. If association churches are not giving on a regular basis, the first step may be to inspire them to give to specific causes. Associational life is very much about trust. The associational mission strategist who can successfully show the results of a one-time gift may foster the necessary trust to transform the "event giver" into a monthly supporter.

> "If association churches are not giving on a regular basis, the first step may be to inspire them to give to specific causes. Associational life is very much about trust."

In-Kind Donations

Seek in-kind donations of goods and services from businesses, individuals, and other organizations. This could include office supplies, event space, pro bono services (e.g., legal or accounting assistance), and professional expertise. In-kind donations can help reduce expenses and stretch limited resources further. Many of the larger box stores have charitable programs to give much-needed supplies or services to non-profit organizations. The application process is usually straightforward and simple. During my tenure at the High Desert Baptist Association, I was able to inspire secular business owners to donate to church planting. How? I sat down with local business owners, some of whom owned businesses that had been victims of crime, and inspired them with the thought of an improved and safer community with a new local church plant ministering nearby. We faithfully recognized these secular donors as having contributed to our mission.

Focus on Impact

Prioritize programs and initiatives that have the greatest potential for positive impact and return on investment. Conduct regular evaluations to assess the effectiveness of programs and make data-driven decisions about resource allocation. If the return on two equally strategic events or actions are dramatically different, opt to continue the one that produces the greater ROI. Pour your time and energies into the greatest win areas.

In the fast-paced world of leadership, it's all too easy to succumb to the "tyranny of the urgent," where pressing tasks clamor for immediate attention, overshadowing the truly important priorities. As a leader, it's essential to discern between the important and the urgent, recognizing that not all demands are of equal significance. While urgent matters may demand immediate action, they often distract from the important, long-term goals that drive meaningful progress and growth. By cultivating discernment and prioritizing tasks based on their alignment with overarching objectives and values, leaders can navigate the constant barrage of urgent demands with clarity and purpose. Embracing this mindset allows leaders to allocate their time, energy, and resources effectively, ensuring that they invest in what truly matters and propel their associations forward amidst the chaos of the urgent.

Capacity Building

Invest in building the capacity of staff and volunteers through training, professional development, and mentorship programs. Developing the skills and expertise of team members can enhance organizational effectiveness and efficiency over the long term. Invite your pastors to participate as well. Once the trust is built, you can encourage these pastors to trust you with the building of their staff and volunteers. I will discuss this in detail in chapter ten, "Engaging Secondary and Tertiary Leaders."

Transparency and Accountability

Maintain transparency in financial management and operations to build trust with donors and stakeholders. Demonstrating accountability and stewardship of resources is essential for sustaining support and credibility. Regular self-prescribed audits play a vital role in bolstering the trust of member churches. By voluntarily conducting thorough examinations of your financial and operational practices, you can demonstrate a commitment to transparency, accountability, and integrity. These audits serve as a proactive measure to identify any areas of concern, ensure compliance with regulatory requirements, and strengthen internal controls. Moreover, they provide an opportunity to communicate openly with member churches, fostering a culture of trust and partnership. Through transparent reporting and diligent oversight, associations can instill confidence in their stewardship of resources and their commitment to upholding the values and mission of the greater Baptist community. As a result, member churches can rest assured that their contributions are being managed responsibly and ethically, further solidifying the bonds of trust within the association.

Additionally, you must let your member churches see that their gifts are creating kingdom impact. You turn the hearts of your people by telling stories, sharing victories, and being authentically vulnerable about the ways in which you anticipate future improvement in stewardship.

Continuous Learning and Adaptation

Embrace a culture of continuous learning and adaptation, where the association regularly reflects on its experiences, learns from both successes and failures, and adapts strategies accordingly. Being flexible and responsive to changing circumstances is key to navigating challenges and maximizing impact over time. Many an associational mission strategist is reluctant to own his failures. We should not be. Public vulnerability can add credibility to you and your ministry. I am part of a generation that wanted to see a flawless leader. We wanted to know that he or she had it all together. The ascending generations (millennials and following) have no such expectation of their leaders. They desire to see a leader who is flawed like them yet working to improve his or her condition. Much has been written of late about these generations' propensity to seek out leaders who are authentically vulnerable, and the associational mission strategist who can grasp these generational expectations can capitalize on this perspective.

These strategies are not—all—for everyone. However, thoughtfully and creatively implementing the strategies that can benefit your association will optimize associational effectiveness and allow you to achieve greater things with limited financial resources.

03
Volunteer Management

Whatever you do, do it from the heart, as something done for the Lord and not for people, knowing that you will receive the reward of an inheritance from the Lord. You serve the Lord Christ.

Colossians 3:23-24

Once upon a time, in a quaint village nestled between rolling hills and whispering streams, there lived a diligent but inexperienced leader named Luca. Luca was tasked with leading a group of volunteers to revitalize their beloved community garden, a once-thriving haven of blossoms and bounty now overrun by weeds and neglect.

Eager to restore the garden to its former glory, Luca rallied the volunteers with enthusiasm and determination. But as they gathered on the first day, chaos ensued. Some volunteers argued over which tasks to prioritize, while others wandered aimlessly, unsure of where to begin. The garden seemed a daunting mess, and Luca felt the weight of doubt creeping into his heart.

Undeterred, Luca knew that true leadership required more than just giving orders. He took a step back, observing the strengths and passions of each volunteer, and sought to inspire them with a vision of what the garden could become. With patience and empathy, he listened to their ideas and concerns, fostering a sense of ownership and collaboration among the group.

As days turned into weeks, Luca's transformational leadership began to bear fruit. He led by example, working alongside the volunteers with unwavering dedication and a smile on his face. He encouraged them to embrace challenges as opportunities for growth and learning, celebrating their achievements no matter how small.

Slowly but surely, the garden began to flourish once again. With Luca's guidance, the volunteers learned to work together harmoniously, each contributing their unique talents and skills to the collective effort. They planted seeds of friendship and camaraderie, nurturing them with laughter, encouragement, and shared purpose.

By the time the first blooms appeared, the garden had been transformed into a vibrant oasis of color and life. The volunteers stood in awe of what they had accomplished together, united by their shared journey of growth and transformation. And at the heart of it all stood Luca, not just as a leader, but as a source of inspiration and hope.

From that day forward, Luca's leadership continued to inspire those around him, igniting a spark of passion and purpose in all who crossed his path. And as the seasons changed and the garden thrived, the villagers came to realize that true leadership isn't just about giving orders—it's about empowering others to rise to their full potential and achieve greatness together.

Enlisting and managing volunteers efficiently is crucial for the success of any Baptist association, as volunteers play a vital role in carrying out the association's mission and serving its members and communities. As we enter this discussion, we cannot dismiss passion and purpose. It is essential for a volunteer to be given responsibilities that align with his or her innate motivations. I will use the analogy of air to represent the life-giving power of assigning volunteers in a strategic manner. Here's why: Just as air is vital for sustaining life, aligning responsibilities with a volunteer's passion or sense of purpose is crucial for sustaining his or her motivation. When volunteers are engaged in tasks that resonate with their interests and values, they are more likely to feel energized, enthusiastic, and committed to their roles. Purpose is one of three key intrinsic motivators that every astute leader learns to leverage for volunteer satisfaction. This intrinsic motivation acts as a driving force, propelling volunteers to actively contribute their time, skills, and efforts to the cause.

This leads to the next important consideration, personal growth and fulfillment. Just as fresh air promotes physical health, responsibilities aligned with passion promote personal growth and fulfillment. When volunteers are given opportunities to pursue activities that align with their passions, they are more likely to experience a sense of fulfillment, accomplishment, and self-discovery. They may uncover hidden talents, develop new skills, and gain valuable experiences that contribute to their personal and professional development. These newfound skills may unexpectedly drive organizational efficiency to new levels.

A sense of purpose also increases engagement and effectiveness. Just as oxygen fuels fire, aligning responsibilities with a sense of purpose fuels the volunteer. Volunteers who feel purposeful about their roles are more likely to be fully engaged, proactive, and resourceful in fulfilling their responsibilities. They are willing to invest time and effort into their tasks, go above and beyond expectations, and find innovative solutions to challenges, ultimately enhancing the organization's overall effectiveness and impact.

Additionally, this approach builds resilience. Just as fresh air strengthens the immune system, responsibilities aligned with purpose build resilience in volunteers. When faced with obstacles or setbacks, volunteers who are deeply connected to their roles are more likely to persevere, adapt, and overcome challenges. Their passion and sense of purpose act as a source of resilience, enabling them to stay motivated, focused, and optimistic even in the face of adversity. Think about the many times volunteers in your association have resigned due to a lack of knowledge, a barrier, or a personality conflict. I can almost guarantee that their duties were not aligned with their passion or sense of purpose, for if they had a sense of purpose, the lack of knowledge would have been met with intellectual pursuit of the answer, the barrier would have been met with problem solving, and the personality conflict would have been met with repeated attempts at reconciliation. This is what passion and purpose foster in the volunteer.

In summary, aligning responsibilities with a volunteer's passion or sense of purpose is essential for sustaining motivation, fostering personal growth, increasing engagement and effectiveness, and building resilience. Just as air is indispensable for sustaining life, passion and purpose are indispensable for sustaining volunteer commitment and contribution to the organization's mission and goals.

Here are some strategies that a Baptist association can use to enlist and manage volunteers effectively:

Clear Volunteer Roles and Expectations

Define clear volunteer roles, responsibilities, and expectations for each position within the association. Ensure that volunteers understand what is required of them, the time commitment involved, and how their contributions align with the association's mission and goals.

It is crucial that we actively promote the myriad opportunities available for volunteering. Without clear communication and invitation, many willing hearts may remain unaware of the ways they can contribute. It's a simple truth: if you don't ask, you won't receive. By spreading the word about your needs and the rewarding experiences that come with serving, you ensure that everyone has the knowledge and opportunity to get involved. This not only strengthens your community but also allows individuals to live out their faith through acts of kindness and service.

Personalized Recruitment

Tailor volunteer recruitment efforts to the interests, skills, and availability of potential volunteers. Identify individuals within the association and wider community who have a passion for the category of need and may be willing to volunteer their time and talents. As stated above, alignment is key to the longevity of volunteers.

A leader must strive to build meaningful relationships with their volunteers, recognizing that understanding their strengths, interests, and motivations is crucial for effective team management. Although it may not always be feasible to form deep connections with every individual, leaders should make a concerted effort to get to know each team member as thoroughly as possible before assigning responsibilities. This approach ensures that tasks are aligned with each person's unique skills and passions, leading to greater job satisfaction and productivity. By investing time in understanding their team, leaders can create a more cohesive, motivated, and efficient working environment where everyone feels valued and appropriately challenged.

Training and Development

Inexperienced leaders may frequently reassign volunteers until they identify tasks at which the volunteers excel. Moving people around until they find their niche can be a precarious strategy that may lead to frustration, decreased morale, and a sense of instability among team members. This trial-and-error approach can result in mismatches between individuals' skills and their assigned tasks, causing inefficiencies and hindering overall productivity. Instead, investing in proper training for the task at hand is a more effective and sustainable solution. Training equips employees or volunteers with the necessary skills and knowledge to succeed in their roles, fostering confidence and competence. By providing targeted training and support, leaders can help their team members excel in their positions from the outset, reducing the need for constant reassignment and creating a more stable and empowered workforce.

Offer workshops, seminars, and resources to enhance volunteers' skills, knowledge, and understanding of the association's mission, values, and procedures. Mastery is the second of three key intrinsic motivators (purpose and autonomy being the other two). Think about this: Why do we play instruments, compete in sports, or learn how to paint or sing? Because the human spirit wants to master the things that interest us. As much as you can offer a path to mastery, you will increase the likelihood of dynamic and sustained volunteerism.

Effective Communication

It's essential to maintain open and transparent communication channels with volunteers to keep them informed, engaged, and motivated. Regular updates on upcoming events, projects, and opportunities for involvement are crucial for fostering a sense of belonging and investment in the association's mission. Utilize a variety of communication platforms, including email, newsletters, social media, and meetings, to ensure that volunteers stay connected and up to date. By keeping volunteers informed about how their contributions are driving forward kingdom momentum and making a tangible impact, you can enhance their sense of accomplishment and fulfillment in their roles. This transparent communication not only strengthens the bond between volunteers and the association but also cultivates a culture of collaboration and shared purpose. As you maintain these communication channels, it's important to introspect and ask yourself how many people in the association actually even know that they can volunteer. Ensuring that volunteer opportunities are widely promoted and accessible to all members is essential for maximizing participation and harnessing the collective talents and passions within the association.

Recognition and Appreciation

Regularly recognize and appreciate volunteers for their contributions and achievements. Express gratitude for their dedication and hard work through personalized thank-you notes, public acknowledgments, awards, and appreciation events. Celebrate milestones and successes together as an association. Find ways to celebrate every step on the way to success.

As I speak at various leadership events, I regularly tell a story of my family in Paris, France. We stood at the base of the Eiffel Tower, and I excitedly informed my middle-school-aged children that we were going to climb the stairs to the top. Their reactions were far less enthusiastic. My daughter glanced longingly at the elevator, then back at me, then back to the elevator, clearly favoring the quicker option. Nevertheless, we began our ascent, step by step. I started counting the steps quietly, reaching around 50 when I turned to see my children trudging along reluctantly.

To liven things up, I counted each step out loud. When I hit 100, I celebrated with an exaggerated dance, raising my arms and shouting, "100! Woohoo!" My children cringed in embarrassment and glanced around to ensure no one else had witnessed my display. Undeterred, I continued, "101, 102, 103…" At step two hundred, I repeated my antics. This time, my children were less embarrassed—they had started counting around step 150. By the time we neared 300, they were racing me, eager to be the first to celebrate. Together, we yelled, "300!"

Finally, at the second landing (674 steps later), my children gazed over the city of Paris in awe. My son remarked, "Dad, look at all the golden roofs." In that moment, I realized something profound. Had I not started counting each step, my children would have been frustrated and exhausted, unable to appreciate the view at the top. By celebrating small victories along the way, they enjoyed the journey and the magnificent view, feeling a shared sense of accomplishment.

Here's what I learned that day: As a leader, I had set the vision for our climb. That's what leaders do; they set the vision for where the organization needs to go. But that vision alone didn't motivate my children. It was celebrating each incremental milestone that made the journey engaging for them. As our excitement grew, we reached our goal with enthusiasm and a sense of triumph.

Empowerment and Delegation

Empower volunteers by delegating meaningful tasks and responsibilities that align with their interests, skills, and expertise. Provide them with autonomy and flexibility to make decisions and take ownership of projects within their areas of responsibility. Autonomy is the third key intrinsic motivator that every leader must learn to leverage. We want to accomplish things with the sense that we were able to make the necessary decisions and—by doing so—accomplish something amazing. This may be an overgeneralization, but there really are two broad categories for leaders: "command and control" or "empower and release." We need to be "empower and release" leaders, especially with volunteers. Nobody likes an overbearing leader watching his or her every move and questioning his or her every decision. A big-picture leader of volunteers learns the importance of accepting results that are sometimes less than the leader expects, encouraging the effort, and setting up a process by which the volunteer can get better in his or her role. This empowerment mindset results in the leveraging of two of the three key motivators— autonomy and mastery—allowing the volunteer to hone his or her skills and do so at his or her own leading.

Team Building and Networking

Foster a sense of community and belonging among volunteers by organizing team-building activities, social events, and networking opportunities. Encourage volunteers to connect with one another, share experiences, and collaborate on projects to build camaraderie and mutual support.

Maintaining strong relationships within volunteer teams is paramount to their cohesion, longevity, and effectiveness. Firstly, relationships foster a sense of belonging and camaraderie among team members. When volunteers feel connected to one another on a personal level, they develop a sense of shared purpose and mutual support that binds them together through challenges and triumphs. These bonds create a supportive and inclusive environment where individuals feel valued, respected, and appreciated for their contributions, thus fostering a positive team culture built on trust and collaboration.

Secondly, relationships facilitate effective communication and teamwork within volunteer teams. When team members have established relationships based on trust and respect, they are more likely to communicate openly, honestly, and constructively with one another. This open communication enables volunteers to share ideas, feedback, and concerns freely, leading to greater transparency, accountability, and problem-solving within the team. Additionally, strong relationships enhance teamwork by promoting cooperation, coordination, and synergy among team members, enabling them to leverage each other's strengths, skills, and perspectives to achieve common goals and objectives effectively. Overall, relationships serve as the foundation for a cohesive and high-performing volunteer team, enabling them to overcome challenges, celebrate successes, and make a positive impact in their association.

Feedback and Evaluation

Seek feedback from volunteers on their experiences, ideas for improvement, and areas of concern. Regularly evaluate volunteer programs, processes, and outcomes to identify strengths and areas for growth. Use feedback and evaluation data to make informed decisions and continuously improve volunteer management practices. Additionally, as the leader, you must be open to hear how your leadership affects the morale of the team. We must not be so closed-minded as to think we are always a positive influence. Feedback and evaluation serve as a two-way tool for associational effectiveness. This serves to foster a culture of continuous improvement and mutual accountability. While it is essential for leadership to provide constructive feedback to employees and volunteers, it is equally important for employees and volunteers to have opportunities to offer feedback on organizational processes, policies, and leadership decisions. This two-way exchange of feedback not only ensures that employees and volunteers feel heard, valued, and empowered to voice their opinions and concerns but also provides leadership with valuable insights into areas for improvement and opportunities for innovation. By creating a culture of open communication and feedback, associations can cultivate trust, transparency, and collaboration among all stakeholders, leading to increased volunteer engagement, productivity, and overall associational success.

Flexibility and Adaptability

Be flexible and adaptable in accommodating volunteers' needs, preferences, and schedules. Offer a variety of volunteer opportunities with different time commitments and levels of involvement to cater to diverse interests and availability. As a leader, it's essential to recognize that volunteers are a valuable gift to the association and should be treated with the utmost respect, appreciation, and care. Volunteers selflessly dedicate their time, skills, and passion to support the association's mission and make a positive impact for the member churches. They are driven by a genuine desire to contribute and serve others, often without expecting anything in return. Therefore, it's vital to acknowledge the significant value that volunteers bring to the association and to express gratitude for their dedication and commitment. Adaptability encourages them to continue their valuable contributions and empowers them to thrive in their roles. Ultimately, treating volunteers as the precious gifts they are not only strengthens the association's capacity to fulfill its mission but also fosters meaningful relationships and a sense of purpose for all involved.

Sustainability Planning

Develop a sustainability plan for volunteer recruitment and retention to ensure the long-term viability of volunteer programs. Invest in succession planning, leadership development, and mentorship initiatives to cultivate a pipeline of future volunteers and leaders within the association.

When a volunteer decides to step down from his or her role, it is often too late to seek a replacement, underscoring the critical importance of having a volunteer pipeline in place. Without a steady stream of potential volunteers identified and engaged beforehand, organizations may find themselves scrambling to fill vacancies, resulting in disruptions to operations and potential gaps in ministry. A volunteer pipeline ensures that there is a pool of qualified individuals who are ready and willing to step into volunteer roles as needed, mitigating the impact of volunteer turnover and enabling seamless transitions when vacancies arise.

04
Missional Alignment

I declare the end from the beginning, and from long ago what is not yet done, saying: my plan will take place, and I will do all my will.

Isaiah 46:10

On the corner of Main St. and Independence Ave., in the heart of a quaint blue-collar town, there was a charitable organization called Beacon of Hope, dedicated to providing support and assistance to those in need. At the helm of Beacon of Hope was a visionary leader named Alyssa, filled with a deep sense of purpose and a bold vision for the organization's future. However, Alyssa knew that to implement the necessary changes and take Beacon of Hope to new heights, she would need to bring her team into missional alignment and transition some employees whose values and skills were no longer aligned with the organization's evolving needs.

With unwavering determination and compassion, Alyssa embarked on a journey to inspire and empower her team, guiding them towards a shared vision of impact and transformation. She began by fostering open and honest communication listening attentively to her team members' concerns and aspirations. Through transparent dialogue and collaboration, Alyssa encouraged her team to embrace change and adapt to new ways of thinking and working.

As Alyssa worked to shift the organizational culture towards one of innovation and excellence, she encountered resistance from some team members who were reluctant to embrace the changes. Old ways die hard. Recognizing the importance of bringing her team into missional alignment, Alyssa approached each individual team member with empathy and understanding, seeking to address their fears and concerns while emphasizing the collective benefits of the organization's new direction.

With patience and perseverance, Alyssa succeeded in shifting the perspectives of her team members, helping them to see the value in aligning with Beacon of Hope's mission and vision. For those whose skills or values no longer aligned with the organization's goals, Alyssa facilitated a compassionate transition process, supporting them in finding new opportunities that better suited their talents and passions.

Through Alyssa's visionary leadership and commitment to fostering missional alignment, Beacon of Hope underwent a remarkable transformation. The organization's team became united in their shared purpose and dedication to making a meaningful difference in the lives of those they served. With renewed focus and energy, Beacon of Hope continued to expand its impact, bringing hope and support to even more individuals and outlying communities in need. And at the heart of it all stood Alyssa, not just as a leader, but as a catalyst for positive change and transformation, inspiring others to embrace their own potential to create a better world.

Like Alyssa, the associational mission strategist holds a position of trust, which can be undermined by poor decisions or strengthened by wise ones. However, missional alignment is more than making good decisions, building trust, implementing change, and communicating well. It is also pragmatic in the sense that something needs to come of it. Alignment without goal-oriented action is senseless. Getting everyone on the same page is no easy task. It takes skill and patience to achieve, setting the stage for forward organizational advance. Let's review some practical ways in which the associational leader can bring his association, his churches, and his people into alignment with God's future vision for their geography.

Associational mission strategists must, without exception, derive their missional imperatives from God Himself. They are entrusted with the sacred responsibility of guiding numerous congregations and influencing the broader faith community. To fulfill this calling, they must seek divine direction through prayer, Scripture, and a deep relationship with God. It is through this intimate connection with the Lord that they receive the vision, wisdom, and guidance necessary to lead effectively. Without grounding their mission in God's will, their efforts risk becoming mere human endeavors, lacking the spiritual power and direction needed to make a lasting impact for the kingdom.

"The long-term effects of leadership modeling are profound and far-reaching, influencing not only the immediate performance of an association but also its culture, values, and sustainability over time."

Moreover, relying on God's guidance ensures that the mission of the association aligns with His greater plan for the church and the world. This divine alignment brings coherence and purpose to their initiatives, fostering unity and spiritual vitality across all affiliated congregations. As leaders look to God for their missional imperatives, they model a profound dependence on Him, inspiring others to do the same. This God-centered approach not only ensures the effectiveness and integrity of their leadership but also cultivates a culture of faithfulness and obedience within the entire association. Thus, the true success of the association's mission lies in its leaders' unwavering commitment to seeking and following God's direction above all else.

Clear Articulation of Mission and Values

It is the responsibility of every associational mission strategist to clearly articulate the association's mission, vision, and core values in a way that resonates with member churches. Ensure that everyone understands the association's purpose, beliefs, and priorities, and how their individual roles contribute to fulfilling the mission. What is the role of the pastor, the lay leader, the volunteer? How do they find a place in the association, and how does the association add value to them or to their roles? If the association exists for their benefit, what does that mean? How will that be lived out on a daily basis? What should the expectations of member churches be?

Regular Communication

Discover and utilize the preferred communication method of every pastor and key leader in your association. Maintain regular communication channels to keep members informed and engaged with the association's mission and activities. Utilize various platforms such as newsletters, emails, social media, and meetings to share updates, testimonies, success stories, and upcoming opportunities for involvement. Celebrate every occurrence that aligns itself with the vision or mission of the association. The old adage is true: You get what you celebrate.

Leadership Modeling

Lead by example through demonstrating a commitment to the association's mission and values in leadership roles. Equip and empower leaders to embody the association's ethos and inspire others to do the same through their words, actions, and decisions. Build a culture that reflects the important values of the association. As the associational mission strategist of the High Desert Baptist Association, my personal mantra of "Everything with excellence" became an associational distinctive. The churches in our association saw this reflected in my actions; if we could not do something with excellence, we did not do it at all. This model was infectious and to this day, I occasionally run into my pastors, and they will frequently ask, "Still doing everything with excellence?" to which I reply, "Absolutely!"

The long-term effects of leadership modeling are profound and far-reaching, influencing not only the immediate performance of an association but also its culture, values, and sustainability over time. Here are several key long-term effects:

Cultural Impact: Leadership modeling shapes the culture of an association by setting the tone for behavior, attitudes, and norms. Leaders who exemplify integrity, accountability, and transparency foster a culture of trust, respect, and ethical conduct among employees, volunteers, and stakeholders. Over time, this culture becomes ingrained in the association's identity, guiding interactions, decision-making, and associational practices for years to come.

Employee and Volunteer Engagement and Retention: Leadership modeling plays a crucial role in employee/volunteer engagement and retention. When leaders demonstrate empathy, appreciation, and genuine concern for their employees' well-being, they foster a sense of belonging, purpose, and loyalty among their team members. This, in turn, leads to higher levels of job satisfaction, productivity, and commitment, reducing turnover and creating a stable and motivated workforce over the long term.

Succession Planning and Development: Effective leadership modeling lays the groundwork for succession planning and leadership development within an association. When leaders serve as positive role models and mentors, they inspire and empower the next generation of leaders to step up and take on greater responsibilities. By nurturing talent, providing opportunities for growth, and sharing their knowledge and expertise, they ensure continuity and sustainability in leadership transitions and associational growth over time.

Associational Performance and Innovation: Leadership modeling drives associational performance and innovation by fostering a culture of continuous improvement, adaptability, and learning. When leaders embrace innovation, risk-taking, and experimentation, they encourage employees and volunteers to think creatively, challenge the status quo, and pursue new ideas and opportunities. This culture of innovation fuels associational agility, resilience, and competitiveness in the long term, enabling the organization to thrive in an ever-changing ministry landscape.

Rebuking an employee or volunteer for trying and failing while attempting something innovative can significantly set back or reverse associational progress. Such actions can create a culture of fear and aversion to risk, discouraging individuals from exploring new ideas or taking bold initiatives. Innovation thrives in environments where creativity is encouraged and mistakes are viewed as opportunities for learning and growth. By punishing those who attempt to innovate and fail, the association risks stifling the very creativity and forward-thinking necessary for advancement. This not only demoralizes the individual involved but also sends a negative message to others, potentially leading to a stagnant associational culture where progress is hindered and the status quo is maintained. Ultimately, this fear of failure can impede the association's ability to adapt, evolve, and achieve its long-term goals.

Reputation and Stakeholder Relationships: Leadership modeling influences the reputation and relationships of an association with its stakeholders, including churches, private donors, partners, and the broader community. When leaders demonstrate integrity, authenticity, and social responsibility in their actions and decisions, they build trust, credibility, and goodwill among stakeholders. This positive reputation not only enhances the association's relevance but also strengthens its relationships with partnering organizations and support networks over time.

Mission-Focused Programming

Develop and promote programs, ministries, and events that align with the association's mission and priorities. Ensure that all activities and initiatives are intentional in advancing the mission and addressing the needs of member churches. As discussed earlier, any programs that would run up against or compete with a program found within a member church should be avoided as a conflict of interest. No association should be seen in competition with a member church. (More on that in chapter nine, "The Association is Not a Church.")

Strategic Partnerships

Cultivate strategic partnerships with churches, ministries, and organizations that share similar values and goals. Collaborate with like-minded partners to leverage resources, expertise, and networks in advancing mutual missions and addressing common challenges. Find partnering organizations whose benefits or services enhance the vision of the association. These partnerships can be a tremendous boon to an association of churches, offering myriad benefits that enhance its capacity to fulfill its mission and serve its community. By forging alliances with like-minded organizations, such as local non-profits, community groups, religious institutions, and for-profit companies, an association can leverage shared resources, expertise, and networks to amplify its impact and reach. Strategic partnerships enable the association to access additional funding opportunities, expand its reach into underserved areas, and implement larger-scale projects or initiatives that would be challenging to undertake alone. Moreover, partnerships facilitate collaboration and knowledge-sharing among diverse stakeholders, fostering innovation, creativity, and best practices that strengthen the association's programs and services. Ultimately, strategic partnerships enable an association to multiply its efforts, extend its influence, and make a more profound and lasting difference in the lives of those it serves.

As an example, in my previous assignment as West Region Director for the North American Mission Board, I fostered relationships with many local business owners. Richard, the owner of the local Avis Car Rental franchise was always looking for trustworthy management or employees, and I was always looking for quality jobs to help church planters and their families land well as they moved into North County San Diego. By partnering together with Richard, he had the assurance that—upon my recommendation—he would be the recipient of a quality employee with a faith that brought character and integrity to the job, and I had the ability to offer a job to anyone seeking to plant a church in the North County of San Diego. A win-win.

Member Engagement and Ownership

Foster a culture of member engagement and ownership by involving member churches in decision-making processes, ministry planning, and implementation. Encourage member churches to take ownership of the association's mission by actively leading, participating in, and contributing to its various programs and initiatives. Sometimes, this requires a shift of thinking. For example, earlier I mentioned that an association should never compete with its churches. I used the example of an evangelism rally. It is one thing for the association to compete with its churches and hold an associational evangelism event. It is another thing to encourage the member churches to work together on an evangelism event with the association's support and empowerment. The first will cost you; the second will build your value and give ownership where it belongs—to the local church.

Accountability and Evaluation

Establish accountability mechanisms to ensure that member churches have a sense of alignment with the association's mission and values. Regularly evaluate individual and collective efforts to assess progress, identify areas for improvement, and celebrate achievements in fulfilling the mission.

An association that lacks accountability to its member churches faces significant dangers that can undermine its integrity, effectiveness, and long-term sustainability. Without mechanisms for accountability, the association may become disconnected from the needs, priorities, and values of its member churches, leading to a loss of trust and credibility among constituents. This disconnect can result in a lack of transparency and oversight in the association's decision-making processes, potentially enabling misuse of resources, financial mismanagement, or ethical lapses. Moreover, without accountability structures in place, member churches may feel marginalized or ignored, leading to disengagement, apathy, and ultimately, withdrawal of support from the association. This lack of accountability not only weakens the association's ability to fulfill its mission but also exposes it to external scrutiny, reputational risks, and potential legal liabilities. Therefore, fostering accountability to member churches is essential for maintaining the integrity, legitimacy, and effectiveness of an association in serving its community and advancing its collective mission.

Prayer and Spiritual Formation

Prioritize prayer and spiritual formation as foundational practices for maintaining missional alignment among member churches. Create opportunities for corporate prayer, intercession, and spiritual reflection to seek God's guidance, discern His will, and renew commitment to the association's mission.

An associational leader who seeks God's guidance in all things plays a pivotal role in fostering spiritual growth, unity, and alignment within the association. By grounding his leadership in prayer, Scripture, and discernment of God's will, such a leader demonstrates humility, faith, and dependence on divine wisdom and direction. This spiritual foundation not only provides the leader with clarity, purpose, and strength in navigating challenges and making decisions but also inspires trust, confidence, and respect among member churches and stakeholders. Moreover, a leader who prioritizes seeking God's guidance sets a powerful example for others to follow, encouraging a culture of prayer, discernment, and reliance on God's providence within the association. Ultimately, by aligning his leadership with God's purposes and values, an associational leader can lead with confidence, integrity, effectiveness, and compassion, guiding the association toward greater unity, impact, and fulfillment of its mission.

Continuous Learning and Adaptation

Foster a culture of continuous learning and adaptation by encouraging member churches and their leadership to grow in their understanding of contemporary issues, cultural contexts, and effective ministry strategies.

Equip members with the knowledge, skills, and resources needed to navigate challenges and seize opportunities in fulfilling the association's mission.

Continuous introspection and adaptation are essential practices for effective leadership. The ability to adapt enables leaders to navigate the complexities of an ever-changing landscape while staying true to the association's calling. Through introspection, leaders can regularly assess their motives, attitudes, and actions in light of biblical principles and spiritual discernment. This self-reflection allows leaders to cultivate humility, authenticity, and self-awareness, acknowledging their strengths, weaknesses, and areas for growth. By embracing a spirit of humility and openness to feedback, leaders create an environment conducive to personal and organizational growth, fostering trust, accountability, and unity among team members.

Furthermore, adaptation is crucial for associations to remain relevant, responsive, and resilient in the face of evolving challenges and opportunities. Leaders must be willing to embrace change, innovation, and creative solutions, continually evaluating and adjusting strategies, programs, and initiatives to meet the dynamic needs of member churches and communities. By staying attuned to emerging trends, best practices, and stakeholder feedback, leaders can proactively identify areas for improvement and adaptation, ensuring that the association remains agile, effective, and impactful in fulfilling its mission of serving and advancing the kingdom of God. Through continuous introspection and adaptation, leaders can lead with wisdom, flexibility, and faithfulness, guiding the association toward greater relevance, vibrancy, and transformative impact in the world.

In conclusion, missional alignment ensures that all aspects of the association, from leadership decisions to programmatic initiatives, are oriented toward fulfilling the association's overarching mission of serving its member churches. When the entire association, including member churches, leadership, and volunteers, is united in its commitment to this mission, it creates a powerful synergy that amplifies the impact of collective efforts. Missional alignment fosters unity, clarity, and purpose within the association, guiding decision-making, resource allocation, and strategic planning toward associational initiatives. Ultimately, missional alignment enables the Baptist association to fulfill its mandate of glorifying God, advancing His kingdom, and equipping and empowering churches to be effective agents of transformation in their communities and beyond.

05
Stakeholder Engagement

Without guidance, a people will fall, but with many counselors there is deliverance.

Proverbs 11:14

In the bustling metropolis of Urbania, there lived a young entrepreneur named Bennett, filled with a burning passion to revolutionize the tech industry with his innovative ideas. Eager to bring his vision to life, Bennett embarked on a journey to form his own startup company but faced a daunting challenge—he had no supporters or investors to back his ambitious venture. Undeterred by the lack of initial support, Bennett turned to the power of communication and networking to make his dream a reality.

Day in and day out, Bennett tirelessly reached out to potential collaborators, investors, and mentors, sharing his vision for a company that would disrupt the industry and change the world. Armed with a compelling pitch and unwavering determination, he attended countless networking events, industry conferences, and startup meetups, making connections and building relationships with anyone who would listen.

Despite facing rejection and skepticism along the way, Bennett remained undaunted, knowing that each conversation brought him one step closer to his goal. Slowly but surely, his persistence began to pay off as supporters and allies began to rally to his cause. Influential industry leaders were drawn to Bennett's passion and vision, offering their expertise, resources, and connections to help bring his startup to life.

With each new supporter who joined his cause, Bennett's company gained momentum and strength. Together, they worked tirelessly to develop groundbreaking products, secure funding, and build a strong team of talented individuals who shared Bennett's vision for innovation and excellence. Through their collective efforts and unwavering dedication, they were able to launch their startup company with great success, making waves in the tech industry and leaving a lasting impact on the world.

In the end, what had started as a lone entrepreneur's dream had blossomed into a thriving organization, with supporters and collaborators from all walks of life coming together to bring Bennett's vision to life. And at the heart of it all stood Bennett, not just as a leader, but as a testament to the power of communication, perseverance, and collaboration to overcome any obstacle and achieve greatness in the modern corporate world.

Ensuring stakeholder engagement is vital for the success and sustainability of the association. "Stakeholder" is a foreign term to many in ministry, so allow me to provide some clarity. A stakeholder is any individual, group, or organization that has an interest in or is affected by the activities and outcomes of the association. This may include board members, employees, volunteers, member churches, donors, beneficiaries, community members, partners, and regulatory bodies. Stakeholders are integral to the association's mission as they contribute resources, support, and influence, and their engagement is crucial for the association's success and sustainability. Here are some strategies that can help achieve stakeholder engagement.

Identify Key Stakeholders

Identify and prioritize stakeholders who have a vested interest in the association's mission, activities, and outcomes. This may include member churches, pastors, congregants, community leaders, donors, partner organizations, businesses, and government agencies. Some may take issue with the identification of stakeholders who do not adhere to the Christian worldview or standards that we do; however, we must not make the mistake of associating the word "stakeholder" with the words "decision maker." Take the government, for example. The church has long sought to supplement the government's attempts to provide social services for the greater good of the community. In these cases, the government was a stakeholder but had no say in the operation or methodologies of the church. Each association must decide to what degree they will work with secular authorities or businesses in support of the association's mission and vision. This is a matter of conscience and conviction that should not be questioned by those outside of the association. It is a decision made by its leaders. I have faith that all associations will be led by the Lord in these issues. One might simply ask, when identifying stakeholders, "Who can help us make this happen?"

Open Communication Channels

Maintain open and transparent communication channels to facilitate dialogue and collaboration with stakeholders. Utilize various platforms such as newsletters, emails, social media, websites, meetings, and forums to share information, updates, and opportunities for engagement.

Listen Actively

Actively listen to the needs, concerns, and feedback of stakeholders to understand their perspectives and priorities. Create opportunities for stakeholders to voice their opinions, ask questions, and contribute ideas for improving the association's programs and services.

Active listening is a fundamental communication skill characterized by fully engaging with and understanding what another person is saying. It involves not only hearing the words spoken but also paying close attention to the speaker's tone, body language, and underlying emotions. Active listening requires individuals to set aside distractions, suspend judgment, and empathize with the speaker's perspective, demonstrating genuine interest and concern for his or her thoughts and feelings. Additionally, active listening entails providing feedback, paraphrasing, and asking clarifying questions to ensure accurate comprehension and demonstrate attentiveness. By practicing active listening, the associational mission strategist can foster deeper connections, build trust, and promote effective communication, leading to more meaningful and productive interactions in personal and professional settings.

Engage in Two-Way Communication

Foster a culture of two-way communication by soliciting input and feedback, as well as responding promptly to inquiries and concerns from stakeholders. Demonstrate a genuine willingness to listen, learn, and collaborate with stakeholders in decision-making processes.

Proactive two-way communication plays a pivotal role in maintaining strong relationships and fostering trust among stakeholders in any organization. By keeping stakeholders regularly informed and up to date on relevant developments, initiatives, and progress, associations demonstrate transparency, accountability, and a commitment to open dialogue. Proactive communication not only helps to prevent misunderstandings, confusion, and misinformation but also empowers stakeholders to feel valued, engaged, and invested in the association's mission and goals. Moreover, by soliciting feedback, input, and perspectives from stakeholders, proactive communication enables associations to make more informed decisions, identify potential challenges or opportunities, and strengthen collaboration and alignment towards shared objectives. Ultimately, proactive communication cultivates a culture of transparency, trust, and partnership, laying the foundation for long-term success and positive relationships with stakeholders.

Collaborative Decision Making

This might appear to contradict my earlier point about not confusing "stakeholder" with "decision maker," but it does not. While the final decisions rest with you, your best advisors are your stakeholders. They offer different perspectives and insights. Engage stakeholders in decision-making processes that impact them by seeking their input, consulting on key issues, and integrating their viewpoints into strategic planning and policy development. Foster consensus and ownership among stakeholders through active involvement in the decision-making process, and then proceed to make your decision.

Collaborative decision-making empowers participants by giving them a sense of ownership and buy-in over the outcomes of the decision. By involving individuals in the decision-making process, associations tap into the diverse perspectives, expertise, and insights of their team members, leading to more well-rounded and informed decisions. When individuals feel heard and valued, they become more invested in the outcomes and are more likely to support and champion the decisions made. Collaborative decision-making fosters a culture of trust, transparency, and accountability, as participants feel a sense of ownership over the decisions and are motivated to work towards their successful implementation. Moreover, by actively engaging in the decision-making process, individuals develop a deeper understanding of the rationale behind the decisions and are more committed to their execution, ultimately leading to increased morale, productivity, and success within the organization.

Transparency and Accountability

Maintain transparency in the association's operations, finances, and decision-making processes to build trust and credibility with stakeholders. Provide regular updates and reports on the association's activities, achievements, challenges, and financial performance to keep stakeholders informed and engaged.

A lack of transparency within an association can create a breeding ground for speculation and distrust among its members. When information is withheld or communication channels are not open, members may feel left in the dark about important decisions, processes, or outcomes. This lack of clarity can lead to assumptions, rumors, and conjecture as individuals attempt to fill in the gaps with their own interpretations. As speculation grows, trust in the association's leadership and decision-making processes erodes, undermining the foundation of mutual respect and cooperation. Without transparency, members may question the motives

> "An environmental void of clarity is an environment that is rich for speculation."

behind the association's actions and feel disconnected from its mission and values. Ultimately, a culture of secrecy can poison the atmosphere within the association, hindering collaboration, stifling innovation, and damaging relationships among its members. An environment void of clarity is an environment that is rich for speculation.

Build Relationships

Invest in building strong relationships with stakeholders based on mutual respect, trust, and collaboration. Take the time to understand their needs, interests, and concerns, and demonstrate a commitment to serving their best interests.

Building strong relationships with associational stakeholders can create a powerful "pull" effect, attracting additional stakeholders and resources to the association. When stakeholders feel valued, heard, and respected, they are more likely to become ambassadors for the association, sharing their positive experiences and advocating for its mission and goals within their networks. As these relationships deepen, stakeholders may actively seek out opportunities to collaborate with the association, contributing their expertise, resources, and networks to advance its initiatives. This "pull" effect not only strengthens the association's credibility and influence but also expands its reach and impact within the community. By prioritizing relationship-building with stakeholders, associations can harness the collective power of their networks to achieve greater success and sustainability in fulfilling their mission.

Customized Engagement Strategies

Tailor engagement strategies to the preferences and needs of different stakeholder groups. Recognize that stakeholders have unique communication preferences, levels of involvement, and priorities, and adjust your engagement efforts accordingly. However, do not confuse tailoring stakeholder engagement with altering the association's missional purpose, vision, or direction—on these, the association must remain steadfast. Developing effective strategies to attract stakeholders is crucial for fostering growth, sustainability, and impact, but it is equally important to ensure that these strategies align with the association's mission, values, and goals. While diversity in approach can be beneficial, pursuing too many strategies or those that diverge from the association's core mission can lead to resource dilution, stakeholder confusion, and operational inefficiencies. Moreover, divergent strategies may create a lack of clarity and focus, hindering the association's ability to effectively communicate its purpose and value to stakeholders. Therefore, associations should prioritize strategies that align with their mission and evaluate their effectiveness in attracting stakeholders while staying true to their overarching goals. This approach ensures that efforts are focused, resources are optimized, and stakeholders are engaged in a meaningful and purposeful way.

Acknowledge and Appreciate

Acknowledge and appreciate the contributions and support of stakeholders through personalized thank-you notes, recognition events, awards, and other gestures of appreciation. Show gratitude for their partnership and commitment to the association's mission. Let them know how they have made a difference.

The notion that "you get what you celebrate" underscores the powerful influence of associational culture on behavior, performance, and outcomes. When an association celebrates and rewards specific behaviors, achievements, and values, it sends a clear message about what is valued and expected within the association. By highlighting and acknowledging successes, innovations, and contributions that align with the association's mission and goals, leaders reinforce desired behaviors and motivate employees, volunteers, and stakeholders to strive for excellence. Conversely, if an association celebrates or rewards behaviors that are counterproductive or detrimental to its objectives, it risks perpetuating a culture that undermines its success. Therefore, by intentionally celebrating and reinforcing behaviors that reflect the association's values and drive towards its vision, leaders can shape a positive and high-performing culture where employees are inspired, engaged, and aligned with the association's mission.

Evaluate and Adapt

Continuously evaluate the levels of stakeholder engagement and solicit feedback from stakeholders on how the engagement processes can be improved. Use feedback and evaluation data to refine engagement strategies, address gaps, and strengthen relationships with stakeholders over time.

An "evaluate and adapt" culture is paramount in an association as it fosters continuous improvement, resilience, and relevance in a rapidly changing landscape. By regularly evaluating performance, processes, and outcomes, associations can identify strengths, weaknesses, and areas for growth, enabling them to adapt their strategies, practices, and initiatives accordingly. This culture of evaluation empowers associations to stay agile, responsive, and forward-thinking, anticipating and addressing challenges and opportunities proactively. Moreover, by embracing a mindset of continuous learning and adaptation, associations can remain innovative, competitive, and impactful, ensuring their ability to meet the evolving needs and expectations of their stakeholders and effectively fulfill their mission over the long term.

By implementing these strategies consistently and intentionally, the association can foster meaningful engagement with stakeholders, build strong partnerships, and mobilize collective action towards achieving its mission and goals.

06
Adapting to Change

Look, I am about to do something new; even now it is coming. Do you not see it? Indeed, I will make a way in the wilderness, rivers in the desert.

Isaiah 43:19

In a symphony of honking horns, bustling crowds, vibrant colors, and tantalizing aromas wafting from street food vendors, there was a small door on a dirty city sidewalk, housing an organization called TechSphere. TechSphere was once a beacon of innovation and success in the tech industry. However, as the years passed, TechSphere began to lose its edge, falling behind competitors and struggling to adapt to rapidly changing market trends. Morale among employees was low, and many feared that the organization was on the brink of collapse.

Amidst this turmoil, there was a young woman named Clara who joined TechSphere as a software engineer fresh out of college. Clara was filled with ambition, creativity, and a relentless drive to make a difference. Despite the prevailing sense of pessimism within the organization, Clara saw an opportunity to turn things around and breathe new life into TechSphere. She was determined.

Drawing on her entrepreneurial spirit and innovative mindset, Clara began to implement bold ideas and initiatives that challenged the status quo. She organized brainstorming sessions, hackathons, and innovation workshops to encourage collaboration and creativity among her colleagues. Clara also leveraged her technical expertise to spearhead the development of cutting-edge software solutions that addressed the organization's most pressing challenges.

At first, Clara's unconventional approach was met with skepticism and resistance from some of her colleagues, who were hesitant to embrace change. However, Clara remained undeterred, believing wholeheartedly in her vision for revitalizing TechSphere. She continued to communicate her ideas with passion and conviction, gradually winning over her skeptics and inspiring others to join her cause.

As Clara's initiatives gained momentum, TechSphere began to undergo a remarkable transformation. Morale among employees improved, and a renewed sense of excitement and optimism permeated the organization. Clara's innovative solutions helped TechSphere regain its competitive edge, attracting new clients and generating significant revenue growth.

To the surprise of her colleagues, Clara's entrepreneurialism and unwavering determination had turned TechSphere's fortunes around, transforming it from a failing organization into a thriving powerhouse in the tech industry. Her story became a testament to the power of vision, creativity, and leadership in driving positive change and revitalizing organizations in times of crisis. And as Clara continued to inspire her colleagues with her passion and innovation, TechSphere's future looked brighter than ever before.

Adapting to change and staying relevant is essential for the long-term success and sustainability of your association. Here are some strategies that can help achieve this:

Continuous Strategic Planning

Conduct regular strategic planning processes to assess internal and external factors affecting the association and identify emerging trends, challenges, and opportunities. Use strategic planning as a dynamic process for setting priorities, defining goals, and adapting strategies to changing circumstances. Perform a yearly SWOT Analysis to identify strengths, weaknesses, opportunities, and threats.[3] Create mobilizations that align themselves to your discoveries. As you plan strategy related to shifting trends, remember to include a future element to your strategy. What will your association look like in five years, in ten years?

Future forecasting is a critical tool for navigating the complexities and uncertainties of the ever-evolving landscape. By systematically analyzing trends, data, and emerging developments, associations can gain valuable insights into potential opportunities and challenges on the horizon. This proactive approach enables associations to anticipate changes in member needs, population dynamics, and external factors, allowing them to develop strategic initiatives and adapt their operations accordingly. Moreover, future forecasting empowers associations to stay ahead of the curve, innovate proactively, and position themselves as thought leaders among their member churches. By embracing future forecasting as an

---

3. The SWOT Analysis is a business strategy tool, and its creation is historically credited to Albert Humphrey in the 1960s, but this attribution remains debatable.

integral part of their strategic planning process, associations can enhance their resilience, agility, and capacity to drive positive change, ensuring their continued relevance and impact in a rapidly changing world.

Flexibility and Agility

Cultivate a culture of flexibility and agility within the association to respond quickly and effectively to changing needs, trends, and opportunities. Empower leaders and members to embrace innovation, experimentation, and risk-taking in pursuit of the association's mission. Many of us remember Hugh Townsend and the Associational Initiatives Team at the North American Mission Board. Hugh was an amazing leader and personal mentor. His background in coaching made him a natural when it came to recruiting talent and leading a team. I was honored to be invited into his initiatives group for the development of many strategic projects. Our group implemented associational assessments, the core competencies leadership training, and several other value-add initiatives for associations. If there is anything that all of us remember from those days, it was Hugh's admonition to create a fast, flexible, focused, and friendly association. Hugh was on to something important. If it takes your association weeks to respond to a need because of some bureaucratic process, you need to kill that process for something more efficient.

Rigidity in procedures within an association can pose significant dangers to its effectiveness and long-term success. When procedures become overly rigid, they can stifle creativity, innovation, and adaptability, hindering the association's ability to respond to changing circumstances and evolving member needs. This inflexibility may lead to missed opportunities for growth, as the association becomes trapped in outdated processes that no longer serve its goals. Moreover, rigid procedures can create frustration and disengagement among member churches, who may feel constrained by bureaucratic red tape and unable to contribute their ideas or expertise effectively. Ultimately, a rigid approach to procedures can impede the association's ability to remain relevant, innovative, and responsive in a dynamic and fast-paced environment.

> "When procedures become overly rigid, they can stifle creativity, innovation, and adaptability, hindering the associations ability to respond to changing circumstances and evolving member needs."

In contrast, a fast, flexible, focused, and friendly approach to getting things done empowers associations to embrace change, seize opportunities, and adapt quickly to new challenges. By streamlining processes and removing unnecessary barriers, associations can foster a culture of agility and responsiveness that enables them to stay ahead of the curve. This flexibility allows the association to pivot swiftly in response to shifting priorities or emerging opportunities, maximizing its ability to innovate and deliver value to its member churches. Additionally, a fast and flexible approach fosters a sense of empowerment and ownership among employees and volunteers, who are encouraged to take initiative, experiment with new ideas, and collaborate across teams to achieve common goals. As a result, associations that prioritize flexibility in their procedures are better equipped to navigate uncertainty, drive growth, and achieve sustainable success in an ever-changing landscape.

Field Research and Analysis

Understanding the current reality of the association's geography is paramount for delivering services that truly meet the needs of member churches. Leaders must stay informed about trends, demographics, and developments in the broader religious landscape and local community to adapt their approaches effectively. This includes actively monitoring shifts in religious demographics, societal attitudes, and community dynamics, as well as conducting market research, surveys, and needs assessments. Developing strategies for impacting a given geography without this deep understanding is akin to shooting in the dark. Without foundational knowledge, leaders risk missing the mark and failing to address the real needs and concerns of the community they seek to serve. Therefore, investing time and resources in thorough research and analysis is essential for developing targeted, relevant initiatives that make a meaningful and lasting impact. Armed with insights into key drivers and influencers, associations can tailor their services, programs, and initiatives to align with the evolving needs and preferences of their member churches, ensuring relevance, effectiveness, and impact.

Conversely, creating strategies without a defined target in mind can lead to wasted resources, missed opportunities, and ineffective outcomes. Without a clear understanding of the current reality and the desired outcomes, associations may find themselves operating in a vacuum, pursuing initiatives that are disconnected from the needs and priorities of their churches. This lack of alignment can result in initiatives that fall short of expectations, fail to generate meaningful results, or even exacerbate existing challenges. Therefore, by grounding their strategic planning efforts in a deep understanding of the current landscape, associations can ensure that their initiatives are purposeful, targeted, and positioned for success in achieving their overarching goals and empowering their member churches for the mission.

Adaptive Leadership

Develop adaptive leadership skills among association leaders and volunteers to navigate uncertainty, complexity, and change effectively. Encourage leaders to be visionary, resilient, and proactive in leading the association through periods of transition and transformation.

Adapting to change is the hallmark of associations that thrive in today's dynamic and rapidly evolving landscape. Rather than resisting change out of fear or uncertainty, forward-thinking associational leaders recognize it as an opportunity for leadership growth, innovation, and adaptation. By adapting to change, associations demonstrate agility, resilience, and a willingness to evolve in response to shifting circumstances and emerging trends. This proactive approach enables associations to stay ahead of the curve, seize new opportunities, and navigate challenges with confidence and creativity. Moreover, embracing change fosters a culture of continuous learning and improvement, where employees and volunteers are empowered to challenge the status quo, experiment with new ideas, and drive positive transformation. Ultimately, organizations that embrace adaptive leadership are better equipped to not only survive but thrive in an ever-changing world, positioning themselves for long-term success and sustainability.

Allowing individuals who refuse to change to maintain their positions can be detrimental to the overall mission and effectiveness of an association. These individuals may resist necessary adaptations, hindering progress, stifling innovation, and impeding growth. Strong leaders recognize the importance of fostering a culture of continuous improvement and adaptability, where all members are willing to embrace change for the greater good. Transitioning such individuals from their positions, while challenging, is often necessary to maintain momentum and ensure the organization remains agile and responsive to evolving needs and challenges. By making tough decisions to address resistance to change, leaders can safeguard the mission and integrity of the association, ultimately positioning it for greater success and impact in the long run.

Collaboration and Partnership

Forge strategic partnerships and collaborations with your churches, ministries, and organizations to leverage resources, expertise, and networks in addressing common challenges and achieving shared goals. It's essential that the association avoids engaging in activities that the churches themselves should be handling, as emphasized earlier in this book. The association should take a supportive role, collaborating with member churches to ensure their success. In a healthy Baptist association, partnership is characterized by a "How can I assist you with this?" attitude rather than a "Can you help the association?" mentality. The former approach fosters trust, while the latter can lead to strained relationships.

True collaboration often involves working behind the scenes, tirelessly contributing without seeking recognition or praise. In the realm of servant leadership, the focus is on empowering and uplifting others rather than seeking associational or personal accolades. Servant leaders prioritize the collective good over individual recognition, embodying humility and selflessness in their approach to leadership. They understand that true success comes from supporting and nurturing the growth and development of their churches, even if it means sacrificing associational or personal recognition in the process. By minimizing self-recognition and placing the needs of member churches first, servant leaders foster a culture of trust, cooperation, and mutual respect, where every individual feels valued and empowered to contribute his or her best. In this way, servant leadership not only cultivates collaboration but also creates a supportive and inclusive environment where everyone has opportunity to thrive and succeed together.

Embrace Technology

Embrace technology and digital tools to enhance communication, outreach, and engagement with members and stakeholders. Leverage social media, websites, email newsletters, and online platforms to connect with diverse audiences and share resources and information. This is a formidable challenge as technology changes daily.

Staying updated on the latest technology advancements while operating on a limited budget requires a strategic and resourceful approach. One effective process for associations to achieve this is through leveraging free or low-cost resources, fostering collaboration, and prioritizing continuous learning. Firstly, associations can utilize online platforms and resources such as webinars, podcasts, and blogs to stay informed about emerging technologies and trends without incurring significant costs. YouTube offers training for every conceivable form of technology, and it is free to the viewer. Additionally, associations can establish partnerships or collaborate with industry experts, universities, or technology-focused organizations to gain access to training, workshops, and knowledge-sharing opportunities at reduced or no cost. Furthermore, associations can create internal knowledge-sharing mechanisms such as peer-to-peer learning groups or cross-functional teams to facilitate the sharing of insights, best practices, and experiences related to technology advancements. The association may not have experts in any given area, but the member churches may. Explore these possibilities. By fostering a culture of continuous learning, resourcefulness, and collaboration, associations can effectively stay updated on the latest technology advancements while maximizing their limited budget.

Innovative Programming

Develop innovative programs, ministries, and initiatives that address emerging needs, trends, and issues within the association and the broader community. Experiment with new approaches, formats, and delivery methods to engage members and reach new audiences. Find someone who is two generations younger than you and ask him or her how he or she consumes information. This simple step will be insightful (and likely challenging). For example, few associations are leveraging social media the way that they should. While it is easy to write off social media for the plague that it is on society, Christian organizations must engage it to tip the scales. I see this as a missional opportunity. In a sea of negative and harmful soundbites, an occasional uplifting voice may hit the mark. Should Jonah not go to Nineveh?

Diversity and Inclusion

Embrace diversity and inclusion within the association by welcoming and valuing individuals from different backgrounds, cultures, and perspectives. Create opportunities for dialogue, learning, and collaboration across diverse groups to foster understanding, unity, and solidarity. In today's world, this is perhaps one of the most necessary steps in bringing quality change to the association.

Hearing from diverse backgrounds is invaluable when making decisions as it brings a rich tapestry of perspectives, experiences, and insights to the table. By engaging individuals from different racial backgrounds, associations can gain a deeper understanding of the unique challenges, needs, and aspirations of their diverse membership base. This diversity of viewpoints enables associations to develop more inclusive policies, programs, and initiatives that reflect the full spectrum of their constituents' experiences and priorities. Similarly, considering perspectives from individuals with varying political affiliations, such as Republicans, Democrats, and Independents, fosters constructive dialogue and consensus-building, helping associations to navigate complex issues and make decisions that resonate with a broader spectrum of members. By embracing diversity across socioeconomic lines, including individuals from both rich and poor backgrounds, associations can ensure that their decisions are informed by the realities and lived experiences of all members of their community, promoting fairness, justice, and solidarity within the organization.

Furthermore, hearing from diverse backgrounds not only enhances the quality and effectiveness of decision-making but also strengthens the fabric of the association as a whole. By actively seeking out and valuing the voices of individuals from different backgrounds, associations demonstrate their commitment to inclusivity, respect, and unity within the organization. Embracing diversity fosters a culture of empathy, understanding, and mutual respect among members, transcending differences and forging deeper connections based on shared values and common goals. Moreover, by intentionally creating spaces for diverse voices to be heard and valued, associations empower individuals to fully participate in the decision-making process, fostering a sense of ownership, belonging, and investment in the organization's mission and vision. Ultimately, by embracing diversity, the Baptist association can unlock the full potential of their collective wisdom, creativity, and strength, driving positive change and transformation in their communities and beyond.

Continuous Learning and Development

Allocate resources to invest in the ongoing learning and development of association leaders, staff, and volunteers through a variety of avenues such as training sessions, workshops, conferences, and other educational opportunities. It's crucial to equip individuals with the knowledge, skills, and resources necessary to not only adapt to change but also to thrive in a constantly evolving environment. From my experience, implementing quarterly leadership enhancement gatherings has proven to be an effective method for driving associational relevance and garnering buy-in from stakeholders. The local association should serve as a central hub for providing "continuing educational units," continuously offering opportunities for learning and growth. By consistently adding value through educational initiatives, the association can foster loyalty and trust among its members, further solidifying its role as a valuable resource within the community.

Continuous learning and development are akin to breath, essential for sustaining life and vitality. Just as we inhale to draw in fresh oxygen and exhale to release carbon dioxide, the process of learning and development allows us to absorb new knowledge, skills, and insights while shedding outdated beliefs, habits, and perspectives. Like breath, learning is a dynamic and cyclical process that nourishes the mind, body, and soul, fueling growth, adaptation, and renewal. Through continuous learning, we expand our horizons, broaden our understanding, and deepen our awareness of the world around us. It is through this ongoing journey of discovery and self-improvement that we enrich our lives, unlock our potential, and contribute to the greater good. Just as breath sustains our physical existence, continuous learning and development sustain our intellectual, emotional, and spiritual well-being, enabling us to thrive and flourish in an ever-changing world.

Below, I have listed several ideas for growth seminars that may benefit the association's member churches. Doubtless, I have missed many. Ask around. What development needs exist in your context?

Pastoral Care Seminar: Focuses on equipping pastors and church leaders with the skills and knowledge to provide effective pastoral care and support to individuals and families within their congregations.

Church Growth and Outreach Seminar: Provides strategies, tools, and best practices for churches to effectively reach and engage with their communities, fostering growth and impact.

Financial Stewardship Workshop: Offers guidance and resources to help churches manage their finances responsibly, budget effectively, and cultivate a culture of generosity among members.

Leadership Development Conference: Designed to develop and empower church leaders at all levels, offering workshops, keynote sessions, and networking opportunities to enhance leadership skills and effectiveness.

Worship Ministry Training: Provides training and resources for worship leaders, musicians, and technical teams to enhance the quality and impact of worship services within churches.

Conflict Resolution and Reconciliation Workshop: Equips church leaders with conflict resolution skills and strategies to address interpersonal conflicts and promote reconciliation and unity within congregations.

Discipleship Training Series: Focuses on discipleship principles and practices, offering practical tools and resources to help churches disciple believers and cultivate spiritual growth.

Family and Marriage Enrichment Seminar: Addresses topics related to family dynamics, parenting, and marital relationships, providing guidance and support to help strengthen families within churches.

Missions and Global Outreach Conference: Highlights opportunities for churches to engage in missions and global outreach, featuring guest speakers, workshops, and testimonies from missionaries and mission organizations.

Technology and Digital Ministry Workshop: Explores ways for churches to leverage technology and digital tools to enhance communication, outreach, discipleship, and ministry effectiveness in the digital age.

Remember, these are for the pastors and leaders in the association. This is a clear example of a practice that, when provided for the pastors and leaders in your member churches, will add value. However, if these were offered to the congregants of your member churches, you are in competition with the church and create a conflict of interest that will undermine trust in the association. In the case that your member churches ask you to provide a session for their people, offer to do it as a church event, not an associational event. This adds values to both the church and the association.

Feedback and Evaluation

Solicit feedback from member churches, stakeholders, and the broader community on the association's programs, services, and initiatives. Regularly evaluate the effectiveness of strategies and activities to identify areas for improvement and innovation. You cannot improve what you do not measure. This leads us to our next chapter, "Measuring Impact."

.

07
Measuring Impact

For we don't dare classify or compare ourselves with some who commend themselves. But in measuring themselves by themselves and comparing themselves to themselves, they lack understanding.

2 Corinthians 10:12

In the polluted and near-dystopian city of Skylight, there was a renowned architectural firm called Horizon Designs, known for its overbearing and grandiose projects that adorned the city skyline. At the heart of Horizon Designs was Ethan, a talented architect with a passion for creating sustainable and environmentally friendly buildings. However, Ethan was disheartened to discover that the firm's building methods often disregarded the impact on the climate, focusing instead on domineering aesthetics and cost-effectiveness.

Despite the prevailing indifference within the firm, Ethan refused to compromise his beliefs and principles. Drawing on his expertise and knowledge, he began to research and implement measures to reduce the environmental footprint of their projects and improve the aesthetics. He collected data on energy consumption, carbon emissions, and sustainable materials, presenting his findings to the firm's leadership with unwavering conviction. He tirelessly measured the impact of previous projects on the city of Skylight and prepared the data. He researched the systems and how they polluted the city. He gathered data on how the bulky and crude architectural style added to the oppressive nature of the inner-city vibe. He organized listening sessions in which he asked residents how they felt about the buildings that stood prominently over their residences. He documented and reported his findings.

At first, Ethan's efforts were met with skepticism and resistance from his colleagues and superiors, who were reluctant to change their established practices. However, Ethan remained steadfast in his belief that architects had a responsibility to prioritize pleasing aesthetics and sustainability while minimizing the ecological impact of their designs.

Using his fortitude of belief and persuasive skills, Ethan continued to advocate for sustainable building practices, tirelessly lobbying for the adoption of green building certifications and environmentally friendly design principles. He organized workshops, seminars, and training sessions to educate his colleagues about the importance of aesthetics and the benefits of incorporating green features into their projects.

Slowly but surely, Ethan's perseverance began to pay off. His colleagues and superiors began to recognize the value of his ideas and the potential for positive impact on both the environment and the firm's reputation. Inspired by Ethan's passion and dedication, Horizon Designs underwent a profound transformation, embracing sustainability as a core value and integrating aesthetically pleasing designs into all their projects.

In the end, Ethan's unwavering commitment had not only changed the direction of Horizon Designs but had also set a new standard for the architectural industry in Skylight. His story became a testament to the power of data, measures, conviction, perseverance, and leadership in driving positive change and creating a more sustainable future for generations to come. And as Horizon Designs continued to lead the way in environmentally friendly design, Ethan's legacy lived on as a beacon of inspiration for architects everywhere.

Measuring impact and significance is crucial for a Baptist association to assess the effectiveness of its programs, services, and initiatives in fulfilling its mission and serving its member churches. We too often measure the unimportant things. The associational mission strategist must learn what to measure so that he may improve the association at all levels. Measuring the right things is essential for effective decision-making, resource allocation, and performance evaluation. When associations focus on meaningful and relevant metrics aligned with their mission, goals, and strategic priorities, they gain valuable insights into their progress, impact, and areas for improvement. However, measuring unimportant or irrelevant metrics can be counterproductive, wasting both time and energy that could be better spent on activities that drive value and advance the association's mission. By identifying and prioritizing key performance indicators that directly contribute to the association's success, leaders can ensure that resources are allocated efficiently, efforts are directed towards high-impact initiatives, and progress is measured accurately. This disciplined approach to measurement not only enhances accountability and transparency but also enables associations to optimize their performance, maximize their impact, and achieve their desired outcomes effectively.

Operating without measures can be a risky proposition for leaders, as it can lead to a lack of accountability and an erosion of trust within the organization. Without clear metrics or benchmarks to assess progress and performance, leaders may struggle to evaluate the effectiveness of their strategies, initiatives, and decisions. This lack of accountability can foster a culture of ambiguity and complacency, where individuals may feel less motivated to take ownership of their responsibilities or strive for excellence. Moreover, without transparent measures in place, member churches may begin to question the integrity and credibility of the leadership, leading to a breakdown in trust and confidence. Therefore, it is essential for leaders to establish clear, relevant, and measurable objectives and performance indicators to ensure accountability, transparency, and trust within the organization. I cannot tell you how many associational Annual Reports I have seen that list the following (or similarly meaningless) items:

- 2,300 miles driven
- 32 sermons preached
- 45 church consultations
- 12 pastor and leader breakfasts
- 2 training conferences

These measures mean very little to member churches. In fact, they may even undermine relevance. The member churches want to see end results of strategic action on the part of their associational mission strategist. Reporting on actions taken may provide a snapshot of the activities and initiatives undertaken by an associational mission strategist, offering insight into the efforts made to achieve his goals. However, measuring the results of these actions goes beyond mere activity reporting, providing a comprehensive assessment of the impact, effectiveness, and outcomes of these efforts. While reporting on actions taken may demonstrate the scope of work completed, measuring results focuses on evaluating the quality, relevance, and success of these actions in relation to the organization's objectives. By analyzing key performance indicators, tracking progress against targets, and assessing outcomes achieved, organizations can gain deeper insights into the effectiveness of their strategies and initiatives, enabling informed decision-making, course correction, and continuous improvement. Measuring results is critical for evaluating performance, driving organizational success, and achieving meaningful impact. Member churches want to celebrate results. Compare the list above to the following list of measures:

Four leadership training seminars resulting in the expansion of leader skillsets and the training of 17 pastors and 23 church leaders. This marks an increase over last year's numbers: 12 pastors and 18 leaders.

Two evangelism training events catalyzing 14 evangelism events in our member churches, resulting in 32 professions of faith. This marks an increase over last year's 6 events with 13 professions of faith.

Summer church planting rally resulting in $23,000 raised and 2 of our member churches committing to be supporting churches. This was an amazing first year effort, setting the bar for next year's church planting rally.

In your associational quest to measure the right things, I hope the following points can help facilitate discussion:

Define Clear Objectives and Outcomes

Clearly define the objectives and intended outcomes of the association's programs, services, and initiatives. Ensure that objectives are specific, measurable, achievable, relevant, and time-bound (SMART), and aligned with the association's mission and goals.[4]

Associational actions without direction and clear objectives are akin to sailing the sea without a system of navigation. Without a clear destination or course plotted, associations risk drifting aimlessly, at the mercy of changing currents and unpredictable winds. Just as a ship needs a captain to chart its course and navigate through the vast expanse of the ocean, associations require a focused associational mission strategist with strategic direction to guide activities and initiatives. Without a defined purpose or strategic focus, associations may find themselves adrift, expending valuable resources and energy without making meaningful progress toward their goals. Therefore, like a sailor relying on navigational tools to steer a steady course, associations must establish clear objectives, priorities, and strategies to navigate the complexities of their operating environment and chart a course towards success, all-the-while reporting every measure toward achieving their goals.

4. SMART goals were outlined by George T. Doran in his article "There's a SMART Way to Write Management's Goals and Objectives," Journal of Management Review, 70 (1981): 35-36.

Develop Key Performance Indicators

Identify key performance indicators (KPIs) and metrics to track progress toward achieving the association's objectives and outcomes.[5] KPIs may include measures such as attendance, participation rates, engagement levels, satisfaction surveys, and outcomes related to spiritual growth, community impact, and transformation. We Southern Baptists are famous for our most prominent KPI, baptisms.

Collect Data Regularly

Establish systems and processes for collecting relevant data and information to assess the impact and significance of the association's activities. This should involve gathering both quantitative and qualitative data. This is the only way to assure a comprehensive understanding of associational advancement. Quantitative data, such as membership numbers, financial metrics, and program participation rates, offer valuable insights into the association's performance and progress in measurable terms. These metrics provide tangible evidence of growth, efficiency, and impact. On the other hand, qualitative measures, including stakeholder feedback, testimonials, event evaluations, and anecdotal

> "By combining both quantitive and qualitative measures, associations can paint a more complete, robust picture of their advancement..."

5. KPIs have been accredited to Frederick Taylor since the early 1900s, according to Cristina M. Giannantonio and Amy E. Hurley-Hanson in their article, "Frederick Winslow Taylor: Reflections on the Relevance of The Principles of Scientific Management 100 Years Later," Journal of Business and Management Vol. 17, 1 (2011): 7.

evidence, provide a deeper understanding of the association's effectiveness and relevance. Qualitative data capture the nuances of stakeholder experiences, perceptions, and satisfaction levels, offering valuable context and insights that quantitative metrics alone cannot provide. By combining both quantitative and qualitative measures, associations can paint a more complete, robust picture of their advancement, enabling them to identify strengths, areas for improvement, and strategic priorities with greater accuracy and clarity.

Use Evaluation Tools and Methods

Utilize evaluation tools and methods to assess the effectiveness and significance of programs and initiatives. This could include pre- and post-program surveys, focus groups, interviews, observation checklists, and feedback forms to gather insights from participants, volunteers, staff, and stakeholders.

A simple event evaluation form can serve as a powerful tool for promoting improvement for a yearly event. By soliciting feedback from participants, and volunteers, the evaluation form provides valuable insights into the strengths and weaknesses of the event, helping organizers identify areas for enhancement. Through questions about event logistics, programming, attendee satisfaction, and suggestions for improvement, the evaluation form captures diverse perspectives and opinions, enabling organizers to gain a comprehensive understanding of the event's impact and effectiveness. Armed with this feedback, organizers can make informed decisions, implement targeted improvements, and refine their planning processes for future iterations of the event, ensuring that each year's event surpasses the last in terms of quality, engagement, and overall success.

Important: One of the most difficult things to do is solicit feedback about your own strengths and weaknesses as the associational mission strategist. It takes a strong person to do this well. The first year I solicited candid feedback, it hurt. However, it was perhaps the single most important and difficult barrier I learned to cross. As an associational mission strategist, I found out that—to some—I was seen as intimidating, while others felt that I did not give my full attention to them in conversation, making them feel unimportant. I AM SO GLAD THAT I LEARNED TO SOLICIT AND ACCEPT CANDID FEEDBACK ABOUT MYSELF. Yes, that sentence is, and will be, the only All Caps sentence in this book. It is that important. Candid, anonymous feedback is painful, but liberating. It is embarrassing yet empowering. Receiving constructive criticism is essential for personal and professional growth as it provides valuable insights and opportunities for improvement. Constructive criticism fosters self-awareness and encourages continuous learning. Constructive criticism offers perspectives and viewpoints that may not have been considered previously, helping individuals to identify blind spots, refine their skills, and enhance their performance. Moreover, by actively seeking and welcoming constructive feedback, individuals demonstrate humility, openness, and a commitment to self-improvement, which can strengthen relationships, build trust, and foster a culture of collaboration and excellence. Ultimately, embracing constructive criticism empowers individuals to reach their full potential.

Anonymity: You cannot solicit candid feedback if it is not anonymous. There are many ways to facilitate anonymity. You can create a web form or a mail-in survey that protects the respondent.

Your people will not tell you what you need to hear if they must sign their name to it. Only your closest friends and spouse are bold enough to do such candid evaluations because they know that your love for them is unconditional. In most leadership environments, this ideal is simply not a reality.

Conduct Program Assessments and Reviews

Conduct regular assessments and reviews of the association's programs and services to evaluate their impact, relevance, and significance. Use evaluation findings to identify strengths, weaknesses, opportunities, and threats (SWOT analysis) and make data-informed decisions about program improvements and resource allocation. Additionally, running programs through the SCAMPER mnemonic may assist the association in gaining insights toward focusing and enhancing those programs.[6] SCAMPER is a creative thinking technique used to stimulate innovation and generate new ideas. It stands for Substitute, Combine, Adapt, Modify, Put to another use, Eliminate, and Reverse. Each letter represents a different approach to problem-solving and idea generation. The reader can easily learn to use this tool with a simple web search. It stands as one of my favorite tools for gaining new perspectives related to systems or actions taken in the context of associational ministry.

Engage in an Associational Evaluation

Involve member churches, volunteers, participants, donors, and community partners in the evaluation process. Seek their input, feedback, and perspectives on the association's activities and their

---

6. Scamper: Games for Imagination Development (St. Frederick, MD: D.O.K. Publishers).

perceived impact and significance. Allow the community to speak in on the contributions made by the association in realms outside of the religious community. Perhaps you have never considered the general public's opinion of your presence in the community. Perhaps they don't even realize what or who you are. This serves as food for thought as you consider the impact that the association has on your local geography.

Share Impact Stories and Testimonials

Share impact stories, testimonials, and success stories to illustrate the significance of the association's work and demonstrate the positive outcomes achieved. Use storytelling as a powerful tool to convey the impact of programs and initiatives on individuals, families, and communities. Certainly, you have observed that every chapter within this book commences with a story. Despite the simplicity, or even predictability of these stories, they serve as a foundation for each chapter. Stories engage the emotive right hemisphere of the brain, preparing it for the logical left-brain content that follows.

Report Findings and Results

This goes back to the idea of measuring the right things. The association must compile evaluation findings and results into comprehensive reports and presentations to communicate the impact and significance of the association's work to member churches, including board members, donors, partners, and the wider community. The effectiveness of an association is never hindered by clarity and transparency.

Continuous Improvement

Use evaluation findings to inform continuous improvement efforts and strategic planning processes. Identify lessons learned, best practices, and areas for innovation to enhance the association's effectiveness, efficiency, and impact over time.

A common cyclical evaluation tool used by associations for continual improvement is the Plan-Do-Check-Act (PDCA) cycle, also known as the Deming Cycle or the Shewhart Cycle.[7] The PDCA cycle consists of four stages: Plan, Do, Check, and Act, which form a continuous loop of improvement. In the Plan phase, associations identify objectives, set goals, and develop action plans based on analysis and assessment of current processes and performance. The Do phase involves implementing the action plans and carrying out the identified improvements. In the Check phase, associations evaluate the results of the implemented changes through data collection, performance metrics, and feedback from member churches and stakeholders. Finally, in the Act phase, associations reflect on the outcomes of the evaluation, identify lessons learned, and make adjustments or revisions to the action plans as needed to further refine processes and achieve better results. The PDCA cycle enables associations to systematically identify areas for improvement, implement changes, monitor progress, and continuously enhance their performance and effectiveness over time.

---

7. This idea was originally developed by American physicist Walter A. Shewhart, according to M. Best and D. Neuhaser's article, "Walter A Shewhart, 1924, and the Hawthorne Factory" Qual Saf Health Care, April, 15(2) (2006): 142-143.

By implementing these strategies systematically and consistently, a Baptist association can effectively measure and demonstrate the impact and significance of its programs, services, and initiatives in fulfilling its mission and serving its member churches.

08
Leadership Succession

Jesus came near and said to them, "All authority has been given to me in heaven and on earth. Go, therefore ..."

Matthew 28:18-19a

Once upon a time, in the competitive city of Prospera, there were two companies: Bright Futures, Inc. and Legacy Builders, Ltd. Both companies were thriving in their respective industries, but their approaches to succession planning couldn't have been more different.

Bright Futures, Inc. was a shining example of foresight and preparation. From its inception, the company's founder, Bryan, had implemented a comprehensive succession plan, training talented individuals within the organization to step into leadership roles when the time came. As a result, when Bryan's entrepreneurial gifting led him to bigger and better things, the transition to new leadership was seamless. The incoming leaders were well-prepared and equipped to uphold the company's values, vision, and culture, ensuring continuity and stability in the organization's operations.

On the other hand, Legacy Builders, Ltd. had neglected to establish a succession plan, believing that the company's success was solely dependent on the vision and expertise of its charismatic founder. When the founder unexpectedly passed away without a clear succession plan in place, chaos ensued within the company. There was confusion, uncertainty, and internal strife as employees grappled with the sudden loss of direction and leadership. Without a designated successor or clear guidance from the top, the company's operations suffered, and morale plummeted as talented employees began to leave in search of more stable opportunities.

As time went on, the contrasting fates of Bright Futures, Inc. and Legacy Builders, Ltd. became apparent. While Bright Futures, Inc. continued to thrive under its new leadership, maintaining its position as a leader in the industry, Legacy Builders, Ltd. struggled to recover from the blow of its founder's passing. The lack of succession planning had left the company vulnerable and ill-prepared for the inevitable changes in leadership, ultimately leading to its downfall.

The cautionary tale of Bright Futures, Inc. and Legacy Builders, Ltd. serves as a stark reminder of the importance of succession planning in ensuring the long-term success and sustainability of associations. While it may seem daunting to contemplate a future without key leaders at the helm, establishing a succession plan is essential for preserving institutional knowledge, continuity, stability, and resilience in the face of unforeseen challenges and transitions.

You would think this goes without saying, but ensuring quality leadership succession is essential for the long-term sustainability and effectiveness of an association. Why then is this one of the most neglected responsibilities among our contemporaries today? The unnecessary energy expenditure by new leadership in the Southern Baptist Convention is remarkable and unfortunate, not to mention that the steep learning curve these leaders face while getting up-to-speed kills organizational momentum. Much of this human expenditure is easily avoided by a strategic succession plan. A carefully crafted succession plan for a Baptist association is a cornerstone of organizational sustainability, continuity, and effectiveness. By proactively identifying and developing future leaders, succession planning ensures a seamless transition of leadership roles, minimizing disruption and uncertainty within the organization. Moreover, succession planning cultivates a culture of leadership development, empowering individuals to grow, excel, and assume greater responsibilities within the association. Through mentorship, training, and professional development opportunities, succession planning nurtures a pipeline of talent, enabling the association to fill key leadership positions with qualified and capable individuals who are aligned with its mission and values. Additionally, a well-designed succession plan provides stability and confidence to member churches, demonstrating the association's commitment to long-term stewardship and ensuring its ability to thrive and fulfill its mission for generations to come. Ultimately, by investing in succession planning, associations can build a legacy of leadership excellence, resilience, and impact that extends far beyond the tenure of any single leader.

Here are some strategies that can help assure smooth transitions and continuity of leadership:

Diligently Seek the Lord's Guidance

While this principle applies to every action described in this book, it is particularly important as it relates to succession planning. In preparing a succession plan for a Baptist association, it is crucial to seek the Lord's guidance throughout the process. The association, entrusted to us to manage, is ultimately an organization established for the glory and movement of God. By earnestly seeking the Lord, we align our plans with His divine will, ensuring that the leadership transition serves His greater purpose. Recognizing that the association's mission is rooted in advancing God's kingdom, we must prioritize prayer and discernment to identify leaders who are spiritually equipped and divinely appointed to carry forward the vision and work of the association. In this way, we honor the sacred trust placed in us and contribute to the continued flourishing of God's work through the association.

Identify and Develop Emerging Leaders

Proactively identify potential leaders within the association who demonstrate the skills, character, and commitment needed to lead effectively. Provide opportunities for emerging leaders to develop their leadership capabilities through mentorship, training programs, leadership development initiatives, and hands-on experiences. Though it wasn't part of any grand plan, I stumbled into the role of associational mission strategist after serving as the association's moderator. It turns out, my predecessor, Ed Adams, handpicked me for the role, recognizing my leadership potential and aiming to train me as his successor. Ed possessed a unique gift for seeing what others overlooked and daring to dream beyond the ordinary. His belief in me, combined with two years of shadowing him as he ministered to our member churches, served as my only training. I owe him a debt of gratitude for that invaluable experience. However, in today's landscape of associational ministry succession, training for candidates must be more deliberate and tailored if they're to step into the role and elevate the organization beyond previous standards.

Succession Planning

Develop a comprehensive succession plan that outlines the process for identifying, training, and transitioning leaders within the association. This plan should include clear criteria for leadership roles, timelines for succession, and strategies for mitigating risks associated with leadership turnover.

Raising a successor within a Baptist Association offers numerous virtues that contribute to the association's long-term sustainability and effectiveness. By cultivating leadership talent from within, associations can harness the unique strengths, values, and institutional knowledge of existing members who are already deeply familiar with the association's culture, mission, and operations. This insider perspective allows for a seamless transition of leadership roles, minimizing disruptions and ensuring continuity in strategic direction and decision-making processes. Additionally, raising a successor from within the association fosters a sense of ownership, loyalty, and commitment among member churches, as they see their peers grow and advance within the organization, inspiring others to invest in their own professional development and leadership journey.

In contrast, bringing in an outsider to fill leadership positions may introduce challenges related to cultural alignment, institutional knowledge, and stakeholder trust. While outsiders may bring fresh perspectives and ideas, they may also face a steep learning curve in understanding the nuances of the association's culture, values, and dynamics. This can lead to resistance, skepticism, or mistrust among existing members, hindering collaboration, morale, and associational cohesion. By raising a successor from within, Baptist associations can harness the strengths and talents of their own members, fostering continuity, unity, and a collective sense of purpose crucial for sustained success and influence. This internal leader can then seek external perspectives to gain insights that an outsider might have otherwise provided. This strategy has been shown to result in shorter transition periods and greater retention of institutional knowledge.

However, it's important to recognize that, although rare, a complete overhaul of leadership may sometimes be essential, necessitating external succession. When the associational environment is toxic or riddled with controversy at every level, hiring from outside the association may be the optimal solution. In such instances, the association should consider appointing an interim leader to address immediate issues, followed by an external hire to provide fresh direction.

Transparent Communication

Maintain transparent communication with member churches, staff, volunteers, and donors about leadership succession plans and processes. Keep stakeholders informed about upcoming leadership transitions, timelines, and the rationale behind leadership decisions to build trust and confidence in the succession process. Allow each to speak into the process giving them a sense of trust that the association is diligently working for the optimal outcomes.

Build a Leadership Pipeline

Create a structured leadership pipeline within the association to facilitate the development and progression of leaders at all levels. The associational mission strategist should inspire the member churches to do the same. Provide opportunities for leadership growth and advancement through leadership roles within committees, task forces, ministries, and special projects.

Leadership pipelines can transform the future of an association by nurturing a steady stream of capable and qualified leaders who are prepared to step into key roles and drive the organization forward. By systematically identifying, developing, and promoting talent from within, leadership pipelines ensure a robust succession plan that minimizes disruptions and ensures continuity in leadership. This proactive approach to leadership development fosters a culture of growth, learning, and accountability, empowering individuals at all levels to take ownership of their professional development and aspire to leadership roles within the association. Ultimately, leadership pipelines are essential for building a sustainable and resilient association that is equipped to navigate challenges, seize opportunities, and set an example for its member churches to follow.

Cross-Training and Knowledge Transfer

Encourage cross-training and knowledge transfer among current and future leaders to ensure continuity of associational knowledge and expertise. Facilitate opportunities for leaders to shadow, collaborate with, and learn from one another to facilitate smooth transitions and minimize disruptions during leadership changes. Many associations have leadership cohorts made up of upcoming leaders in its member churches. Knowledge sharing, best practices, and group processing create an unparalleled learning environment for future leaders.

Leadership Development Programs

Implement ongoing leadership development programs and initiatives to equip leaders with the skills, competencies, and knowledge needed to succeed in their roles. Offer workshops, seminars, retreats, and coaching sessions focused on leadership best practices, conflict resolution, decision-making, and other relevant topics. Several potential seminars were mentioned in chapter six, but the possibilities are endless and should be tailored to the specific culture and environment found in your association.

These leadership development initiatives have a profound trickle-down effect that positively impacts and benefits the local church in several ways. Firstly, these initiatives equip pastors and church leaders with the skills, knowledge, and resources needed to effectively lead and serve their congregations. By providing training, mentorship, and ongoing support, leadership development initiatives empower pastors to enhance their preaching, teaching, and pastoral care abilities, leading to stronger and more vibrant local churches. Additionally, leadership development initiatives promote a culture of collaboration and networking among churches within the association, facilitating the exchange of ideas, best practices, and resources that enrich the ministry and outreach efforts of local congregations. This collaborative environment fosters a sense of unity and solidarity among churches, enabling them to pool their collective talents and resources to address common challenges and pursue shared goals more effectively. Furthermore, leadership development initiatives inspire and empower emerging leaders within local churches, encouraging them to step up and contribute their gifts and talents to the ministry of the church. As these emerging leaders are mentored and equipped through leadership development programs, they become catalysts for growth, innovation, and revitalization within their local congregations, ensuring the continued health and vitality of the local church and new levels of buy-in at the local association.

Diversify Leadership Teams

Cultivate diversity and inclusivity within leadership teams by promoting representation from different demographic backgrounds, perspectives, and experiences. Foster an environment where diverse voices are valued, respected, and empowered to contribute to decision-making and problem-solving processes. Throughout my tenure as a pastor, I held firm to the belief, reinforced by firsthand experience, that in terms of church growth, "You get what you put on stage." I had the privilege of leading multi-ethnic congregations exclusively, and I attribute much of that success to the diverse representation within my leadership team. As an associational mission strategist, it's imperative not to overlook any demographic group within your geographical area. Actively seek out opportunities to diversify your leadership team to better serve and engage with diverse communities.

Even among Christians, race sensitivity remains a significant issue, reflecting broader societal tensions within religious communities. The importance of inclusion often sparks debate, as some view it as unnecessary or detrimental when pursued solely for its own sake. However, the perceptual benefits of true inclusion are substantial. Embracing diversity within Christian communities can lead to richer, more vibrant congregations that reflect the universal nature of Christianity. It fosters a sense of belonging and equality, helping to dismantle long-standing prejudices and promote unity. Moreover, inclusive practices can enhance the spiritual and social fabric of these communities, making them more welcoming and representative of the diverse body of Christ.

Mentorship and Coaching

Establish structured mentorship and coaching initiatives to nurture leaders in their personal and professional growth journeys. Pair emerging leaders with seasoned mentors who can offer valuable guidance, feedback, and support as they navigate their leadership roles within their church and the association. Explore the possibility of establishing a coaching network utilizing individuals within member churches. A strategic associational mission strategist can use his influence to facilitate partnerships between experienced pastors and younger or less experienced counterparts, thereby elevating the quality of leadership across the association. Despite common misconceptions, larger churches can greatly benefit from involvement in such initiatives. I cannot tell you how many times I have heard, "The larger churches don't need us!" This is demonstrably false. Many seasoned pastors are eager to coach and mentor younger colleagues, and by facilitating these connections, the association demonstrates its value and relevance to larger churches, fostering stronger relationships and collective growth.

Incidentally, every leader must have a clear understanding of the differences between mentoring and coaching. Mentoring involves a long-term relationship focused on the overall personal and professional growth the mentee. It is often more informal and holistic, drawing on the mentor's extensive experience to guide and inspire the mentee through various career and leadership challenges. In contrast, coaching is typically a more structured and short-term process aimed at enhancing specific skills or achieving particular goals. Coaches may not need to be experts in the coachee's field but are skilled in asking powerful questions, providing feedback, and facilitating the coachee's self-discovery and problem-solving abilities. While both approaches are valuable, they serve different purposes and require distinct strategies to be effective. Understanding these nuances allows leaders to apply the right approach to foster development and achieve desired outcomes.

Succession Simulations and Scenario Planning

Conduct succession simulations and scenario planning exercises to prepare leaders for potential leadership transitions and challenges. Create opportunities for leaders to practice decision-making, problem-solving, and crisis management in simulated leadership scenarios to build confidence and resilience. You should want the association to continue with hardly a glitch when you are gone. Practice makes perfect.

Regularly practicing a succession plan is akin to building muscle memory for associations, ensuring readiness and resilience when the need for succession arises. Just as athletes train rigorously to ingrain specific movements into their muscle memory, associations must proactively prepare for leadership transitions through regular succession planning exercises. By rehearsing succession scenarios, identifying potential successors, and providing them with opportunities for growth and development, associations can cultivate a culture of preparedness and continuity that enables smooth transitions and minimizes disruptions. Moreover, regular succession planning fosters a mindset of forward-thinking and strategic foresight within the organization, empowering leaders to anticipate and navigate future challenges with confidence and agility. Ultimately, by prioritizing succession planning as a regular practice, associations can strengthen their organizational capacity, enhance their resilience, and ensure their long-term sustainability and success. Additionally, this type of scenario planning serves as inspiration to member churches to do the same.

Evaluation and Feedback

Evaluation and feedback have emerged as recurring themes in multiple chapters throughout this book. We must regularly evaluate the effectiveness of leadership succession processes and outcomes to identify areas for improvement and refinement. Solicit feedback from member churches on their experiences with leadership transitions and succession planning efforts to inform future iterations of the process.

The grass may be greener on the other side, but…

I'll be direct—I firmly advocate for internal succession. It's puzzling that Southern Baptists often lean towards seeking external candidates before exploring internal options. This tendency usually stems from inadequate succession planning within the organization, concerns about known flaws in internal candidates, or the assumption that superior choices exist externally. This mindset needs to shift. While the grass may appear greener elsewhere, it's likely because there's manure there as well!

However, when considering hiring an internal candidate over an external one, it's important to weigh both the benefits and potential drawbacks. An internal candidate brings valuable institutional history and knowledge, understanding the organization's culture, processes, and strategic goals. However, there is also the risk of perpetuating unhealthy or status quo practices that may hinder growth and innovation. To mitigate these risks, an internal candidate must demonstrate creative new thinking and a willingness to challenge existing norms. They should present fresh ideas and a vision for positive change, ensuring that their familiarity with the organization enhances, rather than limits, their effectiveness in the new role. Additionally, the candidate must have a keen understanding of the generational shifts and dynamics that have emerged since the last leader took the reins. This insight is crucial for effectively addressing the diverse needs and perspectives of the current landscape, fostering a more inclusive and forward-thinking associational culture.

By implementing succession strategies proactively and intentionally, a Baptist association can cultivate a robust leadership pipeline, foster smooth leadership transitions, and ensure continuity of quality leadership for years to come.

09

The Association is Not a Church

Do nothing out of selfish ambition or conceit, but in humility consider others as more important than yourselves. Everyone should look not to his own interests, but rather to the interests of others.

Philippians 2:3-4

Once there was a bustling town nestled in the heart of the countryside, where a shrewd and insensitive businessman named Mr. Granger ruled over his domain with an iron fist. Mr. Granger owned the only grocery store in town, and he had always been known for his ruthless tactics and cutthroat business practices. However, his latest scheme shocked the entire community. In a bold move, Mr. Granger decided to compete directly with all his loyal customers by opening his own bakery, hardware store, clothing boutique, and even a restaurant, all within walking distance of his grocery store.

At first, the townspeople were taken aback by Mr. Granger's audacity, but they continued to patronize his business out of convenience and habit because the grocery store was a community gathering point. However, as time went on, they began to feel the pinch of Mr. Granger's monopolistic practices. Small, family-owned businesses that had been a staple of the community for generations began to shutter their doors, unable to compete with the prices and selection offered by Mr. Granger's empire. The once-thriving town square became a ghost town, with boarded-up storefronts and empty streets haunting the landscape. The loss of these beloved businesses took a toll on the fabric of the community, eroding trust, camaraderie, and sense of belonging among its residents. As Mr. Granger's monopoly tightened its grip on the town, many began to yearn for the days when competition thrived, and local businesses flourished, realizing too late the true cost of unchecked greed and ambition.

Finally, as the town members moved away in search of more prosperous opportunities and new environments to establish their businesses, the once prosperous town collapsed. Mr. Granger, still not seeing the folly of his ways, shuttered his last remaining business, the original grocery store. What had once provided nourishment and offered a place of community for the townsfolk was now an empty shell, much like Mr. Granger.

The Baptist association, distinct from a local church, serves a broader role within the faith community, meaning the associational mission strategist is not a pastor. Unlike a pastor who shepherds a single congregation, the associational leader oversees a wide geographical area, addressing the needs and fostering the missions of multiple churches. This role is more akin to that of a missionary, tasked with supporting and equipping churches to carry out their missions effectively. The associational leader must strategize and provide resources across diverse congregations, ensuring alignment with the association's mission while adapting to varying local contexts, ultimately serving as a vital connector and enabler for the collective advancement of the gospel. Remember, the association exists for the benefit of its member churches.

Therefore, the Baptist association should prioritize holding activities that complement rather than compete with the standard activities of its member churches. By doing so, the association can foster a spirit of collaboration, unity, and mutual support within the broader community of believers. Rather than duplicating the efforts of member churches, the association can focus on filling gaps, addressing common challenges, and providing resources and support that enhance the ministry and outreach efforts of local congregations. This approach encourages churches to work together towards shared goals and objectives, leveraging their collective strengths and resources to make a greater impact in their communities.

Furthermore, avoiding competition with member churches allows the association to maintain a position of neutrality and impartiality, ensuring that it remains a trusted and respected partner within the community of churches. By refraining from directly engaging in activities that may overlap with those of member churches, the association can avoid potential conflicts of interest, perceptions of favoritism, or divisiveness within the associational community. Instead, the association can focus on facilitating collaboration, promoting unity, and fostering a spirit of cooperation that strengthens the collective witness of the Baptist community.

Moreover, holding activities that are distinct from the standard activities of member churches allows the association to fulfill its unique role as a catalyst for innovation, learning, and growth within the broader Baptist community. By offering specialized programs, training, and networking opportunities that complement the ministries of member churches, the association can help churches expand their horizons, explore new approaches, and overcome common challenges. This collaborative approach fosters a culture of continuous improvement and shared learning, empowering churches to thrive and adapt in a rapidly changing world while remaining rooted in their shared faith and values.

Competing with member churches can have detrimental ramifications. Doing so will undermine trust, unity, and collaboration within the association. By engaging in activities that directly compete with the ministries and programs of member churches, the association risks alienating its own stakeholders, eroding loyalty, and fracturing the sense of community and shared purpose that binds them together. Moreover, competition between the association and member churches can breed resentment, jealousy, and divisiveness, creating a toxic environment that hampers collective efforts to fulfill the shared mission of spreading the gospel and serving others. Instead of fostering healthy growth and innovation, such competition may lead to a zero-sum game where everyone loses, as resources, energy, and focus are diverted away from collaborative endeavors that could have a more significant impact on advancing the kingdom of God. Therefore, the association must carefully consider the long-term ramifications of competing with its member churches and strive to prioritize unity, cooperation, empowerment, and mutual support in all its activities and initiatives.

> "Competing with member churches can have detrimental ramifications. Doing so will undermine trust, unity, and collaboration within the association."

The mandate to never compete with a member church must be inviolate.

10

Engaging Secondary and Tertiary Leaders

Therefore, as we have opportunity, let us work for the good of all, especially for those who belong to the household of faith.

Galatians 6:10

In an up-and-coming entrepreneurial zone, just outside of the state capital, two businesses thrived side by side, each with its own unique approach to leadership and operations. The first business, a quaint bookstore named Page Turner, was led by a visionary owner who believed in empowering his team. Secondary and tertiary leaders at Page Turner were well-versed in accessing the supply chain, understanding the intricacies of ordering inventory and managing deliveries. When the owner decided to retire and pass the reins to his trusted team, the transition was seamless. With their deep knowledge of the supply chain process, the secondary leaders seamlessly stepped into their new roles, ensuring that Page Turner continued to flourish long after the owner's departure.

On the other side of town stood a small hardware store known as Tools & Trade, where the owner held tight control over every aspect of the business, including access to the supply chain. Unlike Page Turner, where secondary leaders were empowered with knowledge and responsibility, at Tools & Trade, only the owner possessed the critical understanding of how to restock inventory and manage the supply chain. When the owner unexpectedly fell ill and was unable to work, chaos ensued. With no one else equipped to navigate the complexities of the supply chain, Tools & Trade found itself unable to restock inventory and meet customer demands. Despite the best efforts of the remaining staff, the business ultimately folded, leaving behind a vacant storefront and a sense of loss in the community.

In this tale of two businesses, the stark difference in outcomes highlights the importance of sharing knowledge and empowering leaders at all levels. While Page Turner thrived under a culture of collaboration and delegation, Tools & Trade faltered due to its reliance on a single point of failure. The story serves as a powerful reminder of the value of building resilient organizations where knowledge is shared, leadership is distributed, and succession planning is prioritized, ensuring continuity and longevity even in the face of unforeseen challenges.

You now have the opportunity to ponder perhaps the most significant question pertaining to your ministry. The answer might just be a harbinger for the future of your association. What is that question?

Has your ministry, as associational mission strategist, been directed exclusively to the pastors within your association?

If you answered yes, your association might be at risk. Here's why: While focused ministry to your pastors is crucial, and they are—and forever should be—your number one customer, the danger lies in what happens when a pastor leaves. The new leadership might not view the association as relevant, potentially leading to a loss of that church's involvement. You could then enter rescue mode, expending significant energy and time to rebuild the relationship—but why go through all that? The solution is straightforward: Establish deep relationships with the secondary and tertiary leaders in each church. If they recognize the association's value, the church will remain engaged regardless of the pastor's tenure.

In other words, the relationship with secondary and tertiary leaders plays a crucial role in preserving associational membership and continuity when the primary leader departs. These secondary and tertiary leaders often serve as pillars of stability and continuity within their respective churches, possessing a deep understanding of the church's culture, values, operational processes, and associational involvement. By fostering strong relationships with these leaders, the association can ensure that there is a sense of trust, collaboration, and mutual support established long before any leadership transition occurs. This relational approach lays the groundwork for a smooth transition and helps to mitigate the potential disruptions and uncertainties that may arise when the primary leader leaves and a new leader takes his place.

Moreover, building relationships with secondary and tertiary leaders fosters a culture of shared leadership and collective responsibility within the association. When secondary and tertiary leaders feel valued, supported, and connected to the broader Baptist community, they are more likely to remain committed to the association and its mission even in times of transition or change. By nurturing these relationships, the association can tap into the collective wisdom, talents, and resources of its member churches, ensuring that the church's membership remains engaged, active, and invested in the association's activities and initiatives. Ultimately, by prioritizing relationship-building with secondary and tertiary leaders, the association can strengthen its network, enhance its resilience, and preserve its membership base over the long term.

As the associational mission strategist of the High Desert Baptist Association, I initiated secondary leader lunches to engage and add value to this crucial group of servants. These gatherings included lunch, a structured agenda for discussion and learning, and efforts to emphasize the importance and value of the association. However, there was an initial challenge, an elephant in the room: pastors were hesitant to send their secondary and tertiary leaders to these meetings without their presence. Understandably, they had their reasons, and there was noticeable reluctance.

As you consider embarking on a similar initiative, let me offer some advice based on my experience. Have the conversation I learned to have: "Pastor, I encourage you to send your second- and third-level leaders to our monthly association gatherings. They are tailored specifically for them. I assure you that my sole aim is to create an environment focused on supporting you as the lead pastor. My goal is to equip them to be the most effective staff members they can be in service to your church." This approach worked! The apprehension disappeared, and I faithfully kept my promise.

Building relationships with second- and third-tier leaders in member churches is crucial for creating a strong, interconnected Baptist association. The association can organize events like leadership roundtables or networking sessions tailored for these leaders. Such gatherings offer opportunities to share insights, best practices, and challenges, fostering camaraderie and collaboration among these church leaders. These training and development programs align with the interests of secondary and tertiary leaders and provide resources and support for their professional and spiritual growth. By designing such events, the association demonstrates its commitment to their success and empowerment within their respective churches. These programs can cover a range of topics, including leadership skills, ministry training, and personal growth, helping these leaders to enhance their effectiveness and proficiency in their roles.

"Building relationships with second and third-tier leaders in member churches is crucial for creating a strong, interconnected Baptist association."

Furthermore, the association can actively seek input and feedback from secondary and tertiary leaders on key initiatives and decisions. By involving them in the decision-making process, the association shows respect for their expertise and perspective, fostering a sense of ownership and investment in the association's mission and vision. This collaborative approach builds trust and strengthens relationships, laying the foundation for a vibrant and cohesive Baptist community where all leaders feel valued, supported, and connected.

Lastly, in Baptist associations, the strength and vitality of the collective body hinge on the depth of relationships among individual churches and the association. As these relational threads weave their way through the fabric of each congregation, they fortify the entire association, fostering unity, trust, and mutual support. These deep connections enable churches to collaborate more effectively, share resources, and address challenges together, resulting in a robust, resilient, and spiritually thriving community. By nurturing and prioritizing these relationships, Baptist associations can achieve greater impact and fulfill their mission with greater efficiency and grace.

Conclusion
Nothing Good Comes Easy

For our momentary light affliction is producing for us an absolutely incomparable eternal weight of glory. So we do not focus on what is seen, but on what is unseen. For what is seen is temporary, but what is unseen is eternal.

2 Corinthians 4:17-18

Better an open reprimand than concealed love. The wounds of a friend are trustworthy, but the kisses of an enemy are excessive.

Proverbs 27:5-6

The path to greatness is often paved with challenges and obstacles, a testament to the truth that nothing good comes easy. Every worthwhile achievement demands dedication, perseverance, and hard work. It's through overcoming difficulties that we grow stronger, wiser, and more resilient. Each setback becomes a steppingstone, each struggle a lesson, guiding us closer to our dreams. The journey may be arduous, filled with moments of doubt and fatigue, but it's precisely this journey that shapes our character and defines our success. This is God's journey for us. Embracing the struggle, we discover our true potential and the profound satisfaction that comes from earning our triumphs. Remember, the most rewarding victories are those we fought hardest for, proving that the best things in life are worth every bit of effort we invest.

In this book we have explored the challenges and complexities that Baptist associations face in their pursuit of excellence. From navigating leadership transitions to fostering collaboration among member churches, each chapter has offered insights, strategies, and practical tools for overcoming obstacles and achieving success. As we reach the conclusion of this book, it is clear that a journey to associational excellence is not without its trials and tribulations. However, armed with knowledge, determination, and a commitment to growth, Baptist associations have the power to overcome any obstacle that stands in their way ... as long as their eyes gaze forward.

As a young associational mission strategist, I found myself frequently observing the seasoned leaders around me. These were individuals with decades of experience, people I was supposed to look up to and learn from. Yet, with some, what I saw and heard left me deeply concerned. I listened as they reminisced about the past, their conversations filled with lamentations of how things used to be and complaints about how much everything had changed. It seemed that their gaze was perpetually fixed on the rearview mirror, unable to shift forward. Many lamented a cut in funding or decreased giving. Some were angry about organizational shifts and changes that directly affected them. Many were looking for someone to blame for their own mediocrity.

Even at my beginning stages of ministry, as a pastor in my twenties, I knew that this constant dwelling on the past was a fundamental flaw in leadership. These individuals were so absorbed in what once was that they couldn't envision what could be. I knew that true leadership is about looking ahead, embracing change, and guiding others toward a brighter future. But these leaders were stuck, anchored to a time that no longer existed.

I saw the impact of their backward focus. Our greater SBC team lacked unity, direction and motivation, any attempt to innovate or improve was quickly dismissed as unrealistic and unnecessary or met with criticism. Their inability to see beyond the past meant that they had forfeited their ability to inspire their churches to move forward. It was clear to me that an associational leader's role is to chart a course for the future and to instill hope and confidence in the journey ahead—not to spread discontent to their churches and their pastors.

> "We broke from the chains of dependency and came out stronger than before. We found ownership of our reality."

As an associational mission strategist, I knew to lead differently. I focused on understanding the challenges we faced in the present (our association had just learned of our loss of funding) and finding creative solutions to navigate them. I encouraged my pastors to think about where we wanted to go and how we could get there, rather than where we had been. By fostering a forward-looking mindset, I aimed to create an environment where innovation and progress were not just possible, but inevitable. We broke from the chains of dependency and came out stronger than before. We found ownership of our reality.

Through this experience, I learned that while it's important to respect and learn from the past, a leader's true power lies in his ability to envision and guide his team toward the future. I knew that to lead effectively, I had to look ahead and inspire others to follow me into that future, not drag them back into the past or to criticize any other autonomous organization for the decisions they had made in the process of their own reorganization.

I began to distinguish between different types of leaders that were emerging through that time of change. There were those who could set a compelling vision for the future, rally the team around it, and motivate everyone to work towards that common goal. One of my mentors, the late Doyle Braden, was such a man. He took me under his wing and showed by example how to lead. Leaders like Doyle are inspiring. They can see beyond present challenges and imagine what could be. They made people believe in a better tomorrow and worked tirelessly to achieve it.

However, I also noticed another type of leader, the ones who lacked the ability to inspire and create a positive vision for the future. These leaders often took a different approach. Instead of motivating their team with dreams and goals, they would find someone to blame or erect an enemy to fight. Sometimes, these enemies were real, but often, they were fabricated or exaggerated. These leaders found it easier to unite their team against a common foe than to inspire them towards a common vision. By creating an enemy, they provided a sense of purpose and urgency, albeit a negative and destructive one.

I realized that these weaker leaders relied on conflict because it was simpler to generate a fight than to foster hope. It was easier to rally people around what they were against rather than what they were for. This method might have worked in the short term, but it never led to true progress or growth. The organizations led by such leaders were always in a state of battle, never receiving accurate information, never looking forward, always reacting to perceived threats, and alienating themselves from the larger body of brothers and sisters that deeply desired for them to return. Left to themselves, these types of organizations will slowly ebb away. Many did.

In contrast, the great leaders I admired ignored these distractions. They didn't waste time creating or fighting enemies. Instead, they focused on doing powerful things, on building and innovating. They showed that real leadership is about creating, not destroying; about inspiring, not instigating conflict.

These observations shaped my own approach to leadership. I committed to being a leader who looked ahead, who inspired my team with a vision of what we could achieve together. I vowed not to fall into the trap of creating enemies to rally against but to motivate through the power of a shared and positive goal. I understood that while it might be easier to fight an enemy, true greatness comes from ignoring the distractions and focusing on building something extraordinary.

Which type of leader are you?

If you honestly recognize some of these negative aspects in your leadership, remember this:

Father created you to be better than that!

In these pages, we have explored the necessary resilience, innovation, and passion that is needed by Baptist leaders who refuse to be deterred by adversity. We have learned that associational excellence is not a destination but a journey—a continuous process of learning, adaptation, and improvement. As we close our final chapter, let us carry forward the lessons learned and the inspiration gained, knowing that together, we can overcome the obstacles and chart a course towards a future of unparalleled excellence and impact in our geographies.

To all the leaders of Baptist associations, I challenge you to rise to the occasion and fight the good fight with unwavering determination and conviction. In a world filled with challenges and distractions, stay focused on the mission entrusted to you, knowing that your efforts have the power to transform lives and communities. Commit to excellence in all that you do, striving for the highest standards of integrity, stewardship, and service, knowing that you represent not just your association, but the very essence of our heavenly Father's love and grace.

Above all, remember that your calling is a sacred trust, bestowed upon you by our heavenly Father Himself. He called you—by name—for your geography. As leaders, honor Him in all that you do, seeking His wisdom, guidance, and strength as you navigate the complexities of leadership. Let your actions be a testament to His love and grace, and may your leadership be a shining beacon of hope and inspiration to all who follow in your footsteps.

As I conclude this book, I am filled with immense gratitude for you, the reader, who has journeyed alongside me through the pages of *Taming the Lion: Overcoming the Obstacles to Associational Excellence.* Your commitment to learning, growth, and service to your association is truly inspiring, and I am honored to have shared this transformative journey with you. Your dedication to excellence and your unwavering passion for ministry to your pastors and leaders fill me with a deep sense of pride and admiration.

I want to assure you that your work is of immeasurable value, and your impact on the lives of countless individuals and communities cannot be overstated. As leaders, you are at the forefront of shaping the future of the Southern Baptist Convention, and your efforts are a testament to the power of servant leadership and the transformative grace of our heavenly Father. As you continue this journey, may you always remember the profound significance of your ministry, and may you find strength, inspiration, and fulfillment in the knowledge that your work is making a difference in the lives of the pastors and lay leaders whom you serve.

Allow me the honor of finishing with one final story ...

In the heart of a community, not far from where you now sit, there was an association of churches led by a man named Reader. He had inherited the association from his predecessor, and upon assuming leadership, he was met with a myriad of challenges. The association was in disarray, plagued by inefficiency, discord, and a lack of vision. Reader felt overwhelmed and, at times, doubted his own leadership acumen. However, instead of succumbing to despair, Reader made a bold decision. He resolved to train himself to become the best leader the association had ever seen.

Reader embarked on a journey of self-discovery and growth, immersing himself in leadership seminars, seeking mentorship from seasoned leaders, and devouring books on leadership and organizational management. He was relentless in his pursuit of excellence, tirelessly honing his skills and expanding his knowledge. Alongside these efforts, Reader dedicated himself to deepening his spirituality and biblical understanding, recognizing that true leadership is grounded in a strong spiritual foundation. He spent time in prayer, studying Scripture, and participating in theological discussions to enhance his spiritual depth.

With each passing day, Reader grew more confident in his abilities and more determined to lead the association to new heights, firmly rooted in his faith and guided by biblical principles.

As Reader embarked on his journey to transform the association of churches, he quickly realized the importance of relationship building. Reader made it his mission to forge strong connections with pastors, mid-level leaders, and members of the churches within the association. He understood that building trust and rapport was essential for fostering unity and collaboration among the diverse congregations.

Reader began by scheduling regular meetings with pastors and church leaders, seeking to understand their unique challenges, aspirations, and visions for their communities. He listened intently to their concerns, offering support, encouragement, and practical solutions wherever possible. Through these conversations, Reader cultivated an atmosphere of openness and transparency, laying the groundwork for meaningful partnerships and shared goals.

Furthermore, Reader helped organize community events, outreach programs, and fellowship gatherings, all through his local member churches. These events provided opportunities for individuals to connect, forge friendships, and build a sense of belonging within the larger associational family. Reader understood that relationships formed the bedrock of a thriving community, and he spared no effort in nurturing these bonds of fellowship and camaraderie.

As time went on, Reader's dedication to relationship building bore fruit. The churches within the association grew closer, working hand in hand to address common challenges, supporting one another in times of need, and celebrating each other's victories.

Under his guidance, the association underwent a remarkable transformation. Through his visionary leadership, integrity, and unwavering commitment to excellence, Reader inspired his team to embrace change, fostered a culture of collaboration and innovation, and propelled the association to astounding success. Reader's journey from doubt to triumph served as a powerful testament to the transformative power of vision casting, perseverance, dedication, and the relentless pursuit of spirituality and excellence.

God bless you, Reader; you are an inspiration!

B.R. Rick Curtis

What Others are Saying

Taming the Lion emphasizes the collaborative nature of Baptist associations and how they serve as a network to provide resources, support, and guidance to individual churches. Rick's clear and engaging writing makes complex concepts accessible, and his creative examples illustrate the transformative power of strong associational connections. This book is a valuable resource for anyone committed to fostering vibrant, healthy Baptist churches through effective association leadership.

Bob Bumgarner
Executive Director, First Coast Churches
Jacksonville, Florida

Taming the Lion serves as a practical guide for association missionaries seeking to enhance their strategic efforts. Through clear writing and creative examples, Rick simplifies complex concepts, providing valuable insights for fostering healthy and vibrant church communities. This book is an essential read for anyone aiming to improve his association's impact.

Mac Lake
CEO, Multiply Group

Rick has written a relevant and timely book on the work of the associational mission strategist. *Taming the Lion* will be valuable for years to come.

Ricky Thrasher
Statewide Consultant of Associational Missions and Convention Planning, Georgia Baptist Mission Board
Suwanee, Georgia

As a former associational leader, I appreciate the insights and cautions Dr. Curtis highlights in *Taming the Lion*. Churches and pastors today need a transparent leader who is willing to walk with them in clarity of purpose. I still believe the local association has the potential to have the greatest kingdom impact at the local level. *Taming the Lion* offers practical and tangible ways to make this a reality!

Dr. Michael Proud, Jr.
Executive Director, Colorado Baptist General Convention
Denver, Colorado

Rick Curtis is an advocate for associations and associational mission strategists (AMS). It comes through clearly in this book. He offers helpful insights into strategic planning, partnerships, engagement, and alignment. Every AMS will be challenged and inspired to lead his association with excellence while bringing glory to Christ.

Dr. Ray Gentry
President, Southern Baptist Conference of Associational Leaders (SBCAL)

Taming the Lion is a story of thoughts, ideas, and wisdom that creates a great read for any working in or around associational ministry. Drawing from a deep well of knowledge and experience, Rick Curtis does an extraordinary job summarizing a wealth of information in his interesting and easy-to-read book.

Johnny Rumbough
Associational Mission Strategist, Lexington Baptist Association
Lexington, South Carolina

Taming the Lion: Overcoming the Obstacles in Associational Excellence is an indispensable guide for any associational mission strategist (AMS) or supporter of local Baptist Associations within the SBC. With his extensive background in both business and ministry, Rick masterfully employs strategic development principles to address the challenges of cultivating a thriving network of churches dedicated to the Great Commission. His insights on leadership succession and the engagement of secondary leaders are invaluable for achieving excellence within associations. Having witnessed Rick's expertise firsthand through his strategic planning and guidance during a complex merger here in Birmingham, I wholeheartedly endorse him as a thinker, practitioner, and now, an exceptional writer.

Dr. Chris Crain
Association Mission Strategist, Birmingham Metro Baptist Association
Birmingham, Alabama

Rick Curtis has engaged with more associations and associational leaders than anyone I know. His insights into associational life are evident in *Taming the Lion*. Rick encourages associational leaders to act with quiet courage, guiding churches towards trust and cooperation. Drawing from his own experience and the lessons he's learned. Rick provides practical solutions to the challenges associations face today. Rick may have saved the best for last with his chapters entitled, "Leadership Succession," "The Association is Not a Church," and "Engaging Secondary and Tertiary Leaders." These topics are crucial for the health and success of associations.

Glenn Davis
Associational Mission Strategist, Heart of Kansas Southern Baptist Association
Wichita, Kansas

Rick Curtis draws from his lessons learned, curated experiences, and well-told stories to provide an invaluable resource for associational leaders in his book, *Taming the Lion: Overcoming the Obstacles to Associational Excellence*. Writing from years of experience with Baptist associations, Rick offers insights that are crucial for Associational Mission Strategists in today's world. If the association is going to fulfill the role of "the most important entity in the SBC ecosystem (save the local church)," those of us who lead associations need to learn from Rick's lessons in this book. Covering topics from securing necessary resources and volunteers to maintaining the biblical mission and adapting to a changing world, Rick equips associational leaders with the tools they need to succeed now and in the future. We can tame the lion with patient wisdom and gracious persistence. Thanks, Rick—I'll be sharing this one often!

Bob Lowman, Jr.
Executive Director, Metrolina Baptist Association
Charlotte, North Carolina

"Adapting to change is the hallmark of associations that thrive in today's dynamic and rapidly evolving landscape." This sentiment found in the pages of this book comes from the experience of someone who has done the job himself and his widespread exposure to AMS leaders from all across the country. *Taming The Lion* is a necessary resource for thinking and implementing associational strategies for the future. Rick can help restore the roar of your association.

Andy Addis
Pastor, CrossPoint Church
Hutchinson, Kansas

I appreciate Rick's honest evaluation of the challenges that our Baptist associations are facing today. He clearly explains these challenges and the potential consequences of ignoring them. Even more valuable are Rick's practical recommendations, which any association, regardless of size or location, can incorporate to proactively address these issues.

Deryl Lackey
Director, Inland Empire Baptist Association
Ontario, California.

Brother Rick's many years of ministry experience, both in the local church and as a local and national AMS missionary, has enabled him to create a valuable resource at a crucial time for every SBC association. I appreciate how intentionally Rick addresses key obstacles faced by associational mission strategists and provides practical "Next Step" recommendations to overcome them within their associational context. *Taming the Lion* reminds us of the significance of local associations and their role in advancing the gospel collectively. This book will be an essential addition to the leadership toolbox of every AMS for years to come.

Scott Shields
Associational Relations, South Carolina Baptist Convention
Columbia, South Carolina

Dr. Rick Curtis has provided an invaluable service to the churches of our denomination with his book, *Taming the Lion*. By identifying and addressing the obstacles associations face in their pursuit of relevance and meaningful impact, he shares strategies and principles that guide an association toward excellence. As an associational leader, I will keep this book close at hand for reference and will recommend it without reservation to my fellow associational leaders and those who will follow the worthy calling of God to serve His church through the Baptist association.

David W Stokes
Lead Mission Strategist, Central Kentucky Network of Baptists

.

Dr. B.R. Rick Curtis currently serves as the Assistant to the President for Convention and Associational Relations at the North American Mission Board. Alongside his early ministry, he spent fourteen years as a college professor and pursued his passion for entrepreneurship by founding three successful companies in the marketing and communications sector. With nearly forty years of experience as a missionary, church planter, pastor, associational mission strategist, seminary professor, and denominational leader, Dr. Curtis is dedicated to sharing his insights on life, faith, leadership, and integrity in today's challenging and often hostile culture. He holds a Master of Divinity in Biblical Languages and Ancient Near-Eastern History and a Ph.D. in Organizational Leadership.

All social media at: /BRRickCurtis @BRRickCurtis

Published by The North American Mission Board of the Southern Baptist Convention, Inc. 4200 North Point Parkway. Alpharetta, GA 30022-4176. A Southern Baptist entity supported by the Cooperative Program and the Annie Armstrong Easter Offering®.
For general information, call 770-410-6000 or email associations@namb.net.